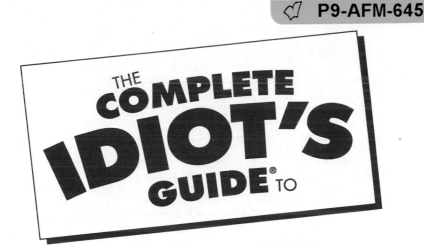

THE COMPLETE IDIOT'S GUIDE® TO

Positive Dog Training

by Pamela Dennison

ALPHA

A member of Penguin Group (USA) Inc.

To U-CD Commander Cody's Great Escape, CGC, A-CD, CDX, NJC, my "crossover" dog: Sorry it took so long for me to find positive training and thank you for being such a patient dog.

Copyright © 2003 by Pamela Dennison

International Standard Book Number: 0-02-864463-8
Library of Congress Catalog Card Number: 2002116796

06   05   04   8   7   6

Interpretation of the printing code: The rightmost number of the first series of numbers is the year of the book's printing; the rightmost number of the second series of numbers is the number of the book's printing. For example, a printing code of 03-1 shows that the first printing occurred in 2003.

Printed in the United States of America

Note: This publication contains the opinions and ideas of its author. It is intended to provide helpful and informative material on the subject matter covered. It is sold with the understanding that the author and publisher are not engaged in rendering professional services in the book. If the reader requires personal assistance or advice, a competent professional should be consulted.

The author and publisher specifically disclaim any responsibility for any liability, loss, or risk, personal or otherwise, which is incurred as a consequence, directly or indirectly, of the use and application of any of the contents of this book.

Publisher: *Marie Butler-Knight*
Product Manager: *Phil Kitchel*
Managing Editor: *Jennifer Chisholm*
Senior Acquisitions Editor: *Mike Sanders*
Development Editor: *Lori Cates Hand*
Production Editor: *Billy Fields*
Copy Editor: *Susan Aufheimer*
Illustrator: *Chris Eliopoulos*
Cover/Book Designer: *Trina Wurst*
Indexer: *Aamir Burki*
Layout/Proofreading: *Megan Douglass, Becky Harmon*

Contents at a Glance

Contents

Foreword

After 25 years of reading, researching, and applying animal training to an assortment of finned, flippered, feathered, and furred critters—from whales to walrus, from dolphins to dogs—I can confidently state that it's finally here: a succinct guide to dog training that explains the often-confusing and complex science of animal learning in simple terms.

Dogs are remarkable animals capable of learning a variety of complex behaviors if owners commit a little time each day and train in small steps using patience and understanding. When they are rewarded for each of these small steps, dogs can learn as fast as dolphins, chimpanzees, or even killer whales. For new pet owners however, training always seems easiest right before they actually bring the new dog home to live. How hard could it be to teach a "Sit," or to walk calmly on a leash, or basic potty training? That is until you realize that the wet spot on the rug is not water, that the neighbors really don't appreciate barking at 2:00 A.M., and that a tug on the leash is supposed to cue your new pet to walk forward and not to go in reverse. As we often learn, what seems simple can get awfully complicated.

Pam Dennison has been a tireless advocate for positive, productive, and enriching training methods, most of which she has outlined in this guide. As a dog-training instructor and award-winning obedience trainer, Pam Dennison has patiently guided dog owners so that they might better understand the process of reducing unwanted behavior in a positive and productive way, while maintaining a trusting relationship with their pet. At the same time, she also teaches dog owners how to shape new behaviors such as basic obedience, potty training, and proper socialization with children. Advanced trainers have also benefited from Pam's expertise, especially in competition obedience training, where her skills are most obvious.

But most notably, she has enough confidence in her personal training knowledge and applied skills to take on some extreme behavior challenges using the same techniques outlined in the following pages. The results have been remarkable. Her success with a highly aggressive Border Collie named "Shadow" has been a shining example of training excellence that quite literally changed Shadow's life. The training that Shadow received transformed him from a severely aggressive and reactive animal to a well-trained and well-mannered pet. Even more remarkable, Shadow is now competing in registered trials and doing excellent!

The rewards of dog ownership become evident when animals are taught behaviors that help them live comfortably and confidently in the household. The relationship between a family and their pet is further strengthened when fascinating behaviors are trained that highlight their pet's intelligence and personality. Finally, true miracles are accomplished when owners learn how to change behaviors in a way that positively impacts the quality of life for animals challenged with overcoming fear, anxiety, phobias, and aggression. In a very practical way, this guide addresses many of these areas and has synthesized the multitude of training techniques into a helpful tool, complete with real examples, entertaining stories, and valuable training exercises. The rest is up to you. Stay positive and keep the training fun!

—Ted Turner
animal behaviorist

Introduction

Thank you for choosing to train your best friend using purely positive techniques! Positive training has been proven by behavioral psychologists to be *the* most effective way to train any behavior. As you will see, punishment causes toxic side effects and can harm your relationship with your dog. There are many, many ways to let your dog know that you don't like his behavior without punishing or yelling at him.

When I started training, I went to a "traditional" punishment-based training class. After a while, I was seeing a decrease of "good" behaviors and an increase of "bad" behaviors with my dogs. They started to hate training and I was angry all of the time.

I was at a standstill in my training for competition because the only advice given in traditional training was to use more and harsher punishment. This made no sense to me and I went on a learning quest, found positive training, "crossed over," and started my business, Positive Motivation Dog Training, in 1996.

For those of you who have trained a dog using traditional methods, it may take a while for you to get the hang of not punishing your dog, but you will see faster results and then be hooked, just like I was!

How to Use This Book

In this book, you'll find everything you need to know about positive training, from where it all began in the laboratory to how to successfully use positive methods in your own home with your own dog.

Part 1, "Positively Amazing: What Is Positive Training and Why Should I Use It?" teaches you the science behind the method, where it all came from, common myths of positive training, and what happens if you use punishment.

Part 2, "Lassie in the Classroom: How Dogs Learn and Communicate," covers how dogs learn, how to respond in a positive way if your dog makes a mistake, the signals dogs give us and how we can use them for better training, and using things the dog already likes as rewards for training.

Part 3, "Let the Games Begin! Positive Training in Action," teaches you how to teach your dog to know his name, look at you adoringly at all times, come when called, sits, down, door etiquette, loose-leash walking, and stays.

Part 4, "The Reality Show: Dogs and Your Lifestyle," discusses how to add a new dog to your household, how to help your dogs and kids get along, and how to deal with "bad" behaviors such as jumping, biting, attention deficit disorder in dogs, stealing, and resource guarding. In addition, this part teaches you how to train while holding down a full-time job and what other options are open for you and your dog once you master basic training.

Extras

Check out the sidebars throughout the book. They're packed full of fun and informative facts:

Pooch Pointers
Tips to help make you a better trainer.

Muttley Meanings
Definitions for technical terms made simple.

Doggie Data
Case studies of real dogs and people and interesting facts you won't want to miss.

Canine Caveats
You'll find warnings here. Ignore at your own risk.

Acknowledgments

My undying gratitude goes to my agent Jacky Sachs and her "bad" dog Roscoe; for without him, we never would have met and this book never would have been written. Many millions of thanks to Jane Killion for her incredible patience and dozens of phone calls ("Jane, will you pick my brain for me?") helping me coalesce my thoughts for this book. To my assistant, Meg Irizarry, for her help in finding great websites.

To my circle of "doggie friends," Ted Turner, Cynthia and John Palmer, Jan and Brian Guz, Patty Ruzzo, and Carolyn Wilki for teaching me so much on the road to positive methods. And for those people who don't even know me, but had a major impact on my life: Leslie Nelson, Bob Bailey, Carol Whitney, and Turid Rugaas.

And to the dogs—mine: Cody, Beau, Shadow, and Mollie and others that have played a role in this book and in my continuing education: Boomer, Sergeant, Mia, Sasha, Bo, Biscuit, Needle, Jazz, Primo, Satch, Ruby, Cherry, Nicky, Dixie, Sirius, Beauty, Tripper, Lucas, and more, many of whom are disguised in this book.

To my mother, Zelda Gross, who said, "Of course you can do it." And to my husband, Jim, for being gracious during the writing of this book to not give me too hard a time about using the kitchen table for my office.

Trademarks

All terms mentioned in this book that are known to be or are suspected of being trademarks or service marks have been appropriately capitalized. Alpha Books and Penguin Group (USA) Inc. cannot attest to the accuracy of this information. Use of a term in this book should not be regarded as affecting the validity of any trademark or service mark.

Part 1 Positively Amazing: What Is Positive Training and Why Should I Use It?

I hope to lead you in the most exciting adventure of your life. Part 1 discusses the science behind the method of positive training, who uses positive training and why, the most common myths about positive training and what happens (proven by science) if you use punishment-based methods to train your dog.

Training your dog should be fun, awesome, and enlightening for both you and your dog. Dog ownership does take time, brain power (not muscle power), and money, but the benefits are enormous in terms of the relationship you have with your chosen "best friend." If you don't have time to train your dog, get a stuffed animal.

Chapter 1

Where Did Positive Training Come From?

In This Chapter

- 🏠 Positive pioneers: Ivan Pavlov and B.F. Skinner
- 🏠 You can't escape the laws of learning
- 🏠 How positive methods came out of the lab and into your living room
- 🏠 The clicker as a positive dog-training technique

Positive training is precise manipulation of favorable consequences (good stuff, like food and toys) in order to get your dog to perform the behaviors you want. The really cool thing is, data from the science of behavioral psychology proves that positive training is successful under the most rigorous conditions, so the methodology in this book is not "just one person's opinion."

"Positive" doesn't equal "permissive." My dogs are subject to strict rules and regulations regarding their behavior around the house and proper manners when we're away from home. I never use physical

4 **Part 1:** Positively Amazing: What Is Positive Training and Why Should I Use It?

or verbal punishment on my dogs. I don't rule by force and my dogs don't rule the roost. I do, however, have some of the best-trained dogs around and have earned multiple obedience titles. My dogs are a pleasure to live with—are yours?

In the Beginning and Beyond: The Origins of Positive Training

We owe Ivan Pavlov, B.F. Skinner, Robert Bailey, Marian Breland-Bailey, Keller Breland, and a host of others a round of applause. Without them, we still wouldn't understand a whole lot about behavior. To fully grasp and embrace positive training, it helps to learn the science behind the methods because without understanding, you and your dog will be two ships passing in the night—something that's not helpful when training your dog.

In the beginning, you might think that theory and history are unimportant (I just want my dog to …); however, the effectiveness of your training will improve if you understand why positive training works.

> **Doggie Data**
> Did you know that Pavlov, a physiologist, was originally studying digestion in dogs but ended up becoming more interested in learning about their behavior?

So let's begin by taking a look at the men and women who were the forerunners of today's positive trainers.

Drooling to Learn: Ivan Pavlov

Ivan Pavlov (1849–1936) is the man who gave us Pavlovian conditioning, also called associative learning and classical conditioning. (Wouldn't it be just too exciting to have a theory named after you?) You remember Pavlov with the dog, the bell, and the drool? Do you remember anything else? Probably not—I know I didn't until I started to train using positive methods.

Pavlov learned through his research that dogs salivated when meat powder was placed in their mouths. He then added a *neutral stimulus* (a metronome) just before he placed the meat powder in the dog's mouth. Once Pavlov had paired the sound of the metronome with the meat powder several times, he turned the metronome on without giving the dog the meat powder, and guess what? The dog began drooling because he knew the metronome meant "food is coming."

So why is this important? Associations are the first steps to learning anything. To bring this closer to home, let's say that you use the word "outside" whenever your dog goes through the door. After a few pairings of the word and the behavior (of going outside), when you say the word "outside," the dog will go to the door.

I discuss more about associative learning in Chapter 5 and show you the extreme significance this has on how dogs learn and how you can use it in training.

 Muttley Meanings
Neutral stimulus refers to something that has no meaning until it is paired with something else either positive or negative.

 Pooch Pointers
Those of you with electric can openers may have had the experience of every pet in the house flying into the kitchen at the sound of the can opener. Wouldn't it be nice if you could get that same enthusiastic reaction, just by calling your dog's name? Well, you can. Read on.

Who Let the Cat Out of the Box: Skinner and Bailey

B.F. Skinner (1904–1990) was a forerunner in the study of operant conditioning, secondary reinforcers, and ratios of reinforcement. For more information, see Chapters 5 and 9. He discovered that changes in behavior are a result of the individual's response (observable behavior) to the events happening in the environment. Learning is the outcome of change in observable behaviors.

And this is critical because? "Observable behavior" is key here because if you can't observe a change in behavior (for better or worse), then you can't know or assume that learning has occurred. We can't read our dog's mind, but we can observe behavior.

Operant conditioning, which is covered in more depth in Chapter 5, is broken down into three sections:

- Antecedent (or cue)
- Behavior
- Consequence

The Laws of Learning

Like gravity, the laws of learning are always in effect. No matter which method you use, be it positive reinforcement or punishment-based methods, the laws of learning remain the same. You can run, but you can't hide! The three basic laws are the following:

- Rewarded behavior gets repeated.
- Ignored behavior stops.
- Once a behavior is in place, variable rewards will strengthen the behavior.

The First Law of Learning

Behavior that is rewarded is most likely to be repeated:

> Your dog mauls you when you come home wearing a clean suit, you pay attention to him (either positively or negatively), and he will continue to maul you whenever you come home.

You might wonder how negative attention (yelling or hitting) could be rewarding for the dog. If the only time you interact with your dog is to tell him what he did wrong, then he'll continue to do those very behaviors. Sounds pretty darned stupid doesn't it? Being yelled at is preferable to being ignored. It isn't as though I don't punish my dogs, but the punishment consists of ignoring them. Because my attention is so positively reinforcing for my dogs, being ignored sends a very strong message that "Mom isn't happy."

The Second Law of Learning

Behavior that is not reinforced will mostly likely stop (extinguish):

> You come home, your dog starts to maul you, and you now ignore the dog for about 10 minutes until he relaxes, and then you pay attention to him.

Now when you come home, he will lie down and relax until you come over to greet him.

The Third Law of Learning

Once a behavior is established, a variable schedule of reinforcement will make the behavior stronger:

> You come home and are now wearing old clothes so you allow the dog to jump on you, but you ignore the dog when you're wearing a suit.

Guess what? Your dog isn't a fashion critic and will continue to maul you when you come home, because you are variably (sometimes yes and sometimes no) reinforcing the jumping.

Unlike associative learning, where a natural behavior (like salivating for food) is now associated with a new stimulus (the metronome), operant conditioning is the rewarding of a partial behavior or a random act that resembles the desired end behavior.

Eureka! Variable Reinforcement

In the days before prepackaged rat food, Skinner noticed that he would run low in the middle of an experiment. Because he had to make his own food, he decided that he would reduce the number of reinforcements given for a particular behavior. Skinner discovered that the rats continued to perform their behaviors at a consistent rate. Behold the discovery of schedules of reinforcement!

Using and understanding variable reinforcement schedules are vital in teaching longer and stronger behavior patterns. Gambling casinos know this, which is why they make so much money on slot machines. Think they just made up the idea of slot machines? Think again! They have scientifically determined the optimum reward schedule—they let you win just enough to keep you hooked! Brilliant!

Doggie Data

The most notable role models for positive methods are the trainers at SeaWorld parks. They train a killer whale to stay still for dental work without novocaine, to urinate on command into a paper cup, to allow blood to be drawn, and many other behaviors needed for animal husbandry. Use punishment on these animals and you'll see the need for new trainers increase because all of the old trainers will be dead. So they use positive training by necessity.

It takes only nine months to train a new whale, including name recognition, come, allowing touching, and daily animal husbandry (how many of your dogs don't allow grooming?), eye contact, not eating the trainer or other animals—even prey—plus all of the behaviors needed for the show.

Rin Tin Tin to the Rescue: Dog Trainers and Positive Training

There are many reasons why people with dogs come to positive training. Some had bad experiences using punishment; some are just curious; and some dogs have behavioral problems that have only escalated as the owner used more and more force and so-called "discipline," leaving the owner nowhere else to turn.

Some people say "I don't train my kids using punishment, why should I train my dog that way?" Why some people seem to think that a 25-pound Sheltie needs more punishment than an 8,000-pound killer whale at SeaWorld is beyond me.

Doggie Data

All of the animals used for commercials, TV shows, and movies are trained using positive methods. Do they sometimes make mistakes? Sure they do, but how many "bloopers" shows are based on the animals? None that I've ever seen, but there are tons based on the mistakes that we humans make. (Although there was one funny take with the dog from *Frasier* where the humans kept making mistakes and the dog finally gave up and started licking his private areas.)

The trainers of these animals just wouldn't get the precise behaviors needed during grueling schedules if they used punishment. Camera and production crews don't want to hear that the *dog* is holding up production.

What Is This Clicker Training Thing?

Clicker training is one facet of positive training that uses a signal to tell the dog that he did something right. A clicker is simply a marker signal—a specific sound that marks the correct behavior the instant the dog performs it. We make the sound of the click valuable by borrowing Pavlov's metronome idea—by association.

The clicker itself is a small plastic box with a metal tongue that when pressed creates a "click" sound. They can be found in most larger pet and dog-equipment stores.

Pooch Pointers

To "prime" the clicker, you can click it and then, within one-half second, feed the dog a treat. Repeat for a solid two minutes—click/treat, click/treat, and so on. Usually within that time, the dog understands that click means food is coming.

Step-by-step instructions for using a clicker for teaching specific behaviors are addressed in Chapters 10, 11, and 12.

Doggie Data _____

Training using a secondary reinforcer such as a clicker was invented more than 70 years ago by B.F. Skinner. Keller Breland and Marian Breland-Bailey (a student of Skinner's) first coined the phrase "bridging stimulus," which later changed to just "bridge." I find it's easier to use the word "marker." Use of secondary reinforcers first became widespread in marine mammal training.

Since I mention a secondary reinforcer, you might wonder what the first reinforcer is. Primary reinforcers are things that the animal doesn't have to learn to like—the animal naturally likes them. Animals behave in certain ways for three basic reasons: to find food, to find water, and to get access to sex. We can tap into these basic needs to make our marker signal (and our relationship) more valuable.

Bridges have been used with marine mammals since the 1950s. Although marine mammal trainers use a whistle instead of a clicker to mark the correct behavior, the principle is the same. Click what you like, reward it, and ignore what you don't want. The clicker imparts valuable, precise information from you to the dog, something that is lacking in traditional types of training.

Clicker training (positive training and clicker training are used interchangeably in this book) teaches dogs to *think* and to use the wonderful, creative brains that they have. It also teaches them that they do have some control. (By "control," I don't mean in a dominating, pushy way, but in a way that brings their own propensities into the training process.) Once you start training using the clicker, you'll see that your dog isn't working for the food—he's working to get you to click.

(Photo by P. Dennison)

A Bull Terrier retrieving a dumbbell.

To illustrate, Laura was teaching her dog, Mollie, to retrieve a dumbbell. Mollie was touching the dumbbell with her nose, I was clicking, and Laura was treating. After a few repetitions, I wanted to raise the *criteria* and have Mollie start to open her mouth for the dumbbell. She touched it with her nose. I didn't click. She touched it again with her nose and deliberately looked at me with this look that only a dog can have, as if to say "Are you going to click or *not?!*" I did not. She looked at me, looked at Laura, and then went to the dumbbell and opened her mouth a tiny bit. I clicked, and Laura treated.

Muttley Meanings
Criteria are the behaviors you will accept from your dog during a particular training session.

It's Not the Dog, Silly

The clicker also imparts valuable information to the trainer. When we try to mark the behavior with words, such as the ever-popular

12 **Part 1:** Positively Amazing: What Is Positive Training and Why Should I Use It?

"good dog," it's hard to tell whether or not we're late in marking the behavior.

With the clicker, we can easily tell when we're late, which will help us to then fix our timing. If we have been continuously late with our verbal "good dog," then we can pretty much assume that our dogs are confused and probably not "getting it." Then we wrongly think that our dogs are stupid, when in fact, we were the ones that weren't clear.

Positive training takes the onus off of the dog and puts it squarely where it belongs—on us. The dog is never wrong. Really. We're the teachers. We're the ones in the driver's seat. When we make a wrong turn and get lost, we can't blame the person next to us because we were the ones holding the wheel. (Unless, of course, it was your spouse telling you to make the wrong turn.)

A few correct repetitions does not a learned behavior make. And if the dog does a wrong behavior, so what? We all make mistakes or do stupid things—even when we know better. I'm allergic to certain foods, but I eat them anyway. And I sometimes say stupid things (insert foot in mouth).

Canine Caveats

Don't assume your dog is stupid. Your dog is probably confused by the mixed signals you're giving him.

Pooch Pointers

Positive training gives us freedom—no more punishment, no more drilling, no more blaming the dog for not doing something that we didn't take the time to truly teach.

Clicker training is all about a change of mental attitude. Clicker trainers have learned to use their brains to train specific behaviors, rather than use pain to elicit those same behaviors. The result? Happier dogs, happier trainers, better relationships, and fewer behavioral problems.

The Least You Need to Know

🏠 Positive training is not mindless permissiveness.

🏠 There are two facets to learning—operant conditioning and associative learning.

🏠 The laws of learning, like gravity, are always in effect.

🏠 Turn your dog into a gambling fool—and a well-behaved dog—using variable reinforcements.

Chapter **2**

Positive Training Fundamentals

In This Chapter

- 🏠 The basic principles and rules of positive training
- 🏠 Positive is easier and faster than punishment
- 🏠 Positive methods create no bad side effects
- 🏠 Teach your dog in small, successful steps

If you are so inclined, you can certainly use old-fashioned elbow grease and spend many hours to clean your oven, because "that's how your mother used to do it"; or you can use an oven cleaner, make your job easier, and have more time to go out and have fun.

You can undoubtedly train your dog using traditional techniques, utilizing punishment, physical manipulation, and intimidation, "because that's the way everyone trains dogs"; or you can use positive methods and have more time to go out and have fun. And because you now have a well-trained dog, you might actually be able to take him with you!

Positive Policies

There are a few simple rules to using positive methods, and of course, they sound too simplistic to really be effective. When you start, the routine might seem insurmountable. Once you get the hang of positive training, it all becomes more natural and second nature.

Reinforce What You Like

You'd be surprised how many people don't know what they want in terms of their dog's behavior. If you don't know what you want, then you won't recognize it when you get it! "I just want a good dog" doesn't count. You may want a dog that doesn't pull on the leash or jump on strangers or try to set his own place at the dinner table. Learn to be more specific.

Make a list of the behaviors you observe in your dog now, along with what you'd rather see instead. Here's an example:

Existing Behavior	What I Want Instead
Jumping on strangers	Sitting politely for petting
Pulling on the leash	Walking calmly by my side
Barking at the doorbell	Quiet when doorbell rings
Bucking bronco for grooming	Standing still for grooming
Growling at strangers	Watching strangers calmly

Once you've identified what you want, you'll be surprised at how often you actually do get these behaviors—even without training. No dog can be "bad" 24 hours a day, seven days a week. Really. Not even yours. And now you can start reinforcing the "good" behaviors because you know what to look for.

For instance, your dog is rearranging the furniture in nightly "puppy zoomies," where he runs around and around, completely out of control, sliding into furniture and knocking over lamps. Why not reinforce him when he's lying down being quiet? Behavior that is positively rewarded will be repeated. Reward him for lying down and ignore puppy zoomies. As long as he's getting proper exercise, he'll lie down more often as a result.

Ignore What You Don't Like

Easier said than done. Now that you know what you do want, I'm sure you know what you don't want. You can address the unwanted behaviors in a few ways:

- Completely and utterly ignore them—simply walk away, go into another room, or leave the house.

- Redirect the dog to a behavior you can then positively reinforce.

- Manage the situation better by putting the dog away *before* he starts driving you crazy.

Canine Caveats

When you're redirecting the dog to a better behavior, be careful. You don't want to accidentally reinforce the dog for doing the "bad" behavior. For instance, you're busy and can't pay attention to your dog, so he then nips you or bothers you in inappropriate ways. You then redirect to a toy. What has your dog learned? "Bother Mom and Dad and they will play with me."

This is how you should properly handle redirection: Dog is bothering you? Ask for an incompatible behavior—sits or downs usually work well for most situations. Count to five while the dog remains in position. *Then* redirect the dog. This way, the dog associates "sit calmly and I get attention," rather than "be annoying and I get attention."

Pooch Pointers

Crate training is not only *not* cruel, but it's an important part of the dog's comfort and security. Teaching this important skill is addressed in Chapter 16.

What if you can't watch the dog because you're preparing a sit-down dinner for 50 people and he wants to sample the menu to make sure no one gets poisoned (such a selfless doggie!)? Put him in his crate beforehand with a nice juicy bone, and voila! Uncle Ben's Instant Good Dog!

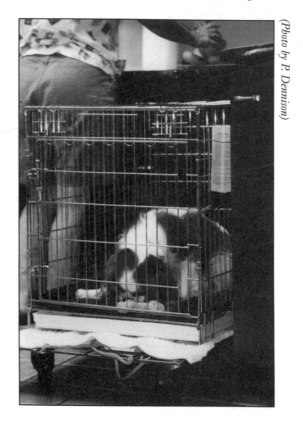

(Photo by P. Dennison)

This dog is in his crate, happily chewing a bone.

Break Down Each Behavior into Tiny Pieces (Approximations)

Breaking behaviors into small segments, rather than lumping big chunks of behaviors together, makes it easier for the dog to understand. Be a splitter, not a lumper. "Splitting" in this case is not the act of splitting up rough play, which is a precursor signal that is discussed in Chapter 7.

For instance, even the behavior of sitting can be broken down into many steps or *approximations:*

  🏠 Head up

  🏠 Head up and back legs slightly bent

  🏠 Head up and back legs bent even more

  🏠 Head up and hind end almost lowered to the ground

  🏠 Head up and hind end hits the ground in the sit position

 Muttley Meanings
Approximations are small steps that make up a final behavior; **splitting** behaviors means breaking them into many small steps and having the dog master one before going on to the next. If you try to combine huge portions of a behavior all at the same time, you're **lumping** those behaviors.

Lumping is when you try to combine huge portions of a behavior all at the same time. For instance, trying to get a dog to walk on a loose leash for a mile the first time you put a leash on him.

Splitting is the proper way to teach any behavior and goes hand in hand with approximation. Start by teaching the dog to look at you while on leash, then move to one step of loose-leash walking, then two steps, then three, and so on. (In-depth instructions for teaching loose-leash walking are in Chapter 13.)

"So that the dog can understand" is key here. You may think the behavior is easy, but perhaps your dog doesn't think so. Remember when you first learned to write with a pencil? The teacher didn't hand you a pencil and then start straight in teaching you to write. He or she probably taught you how to hold the pencil first, making sure it was comfortable for you, and taught you the proper body posture while holding the pencil. The next step may have been tracing letters or numbers until you felt comfortable to go it alone, without tracing. The teacher might have even helped you by holding your hand.

> **Pooch Pointers**
>
> The best approach when teaching a new behavior is to write down what the finished product is going to look like and then break it down into tiny pieces. If at any point your dog seems stuck, then your approximation was probably too large. If a behavior falls apart, go back a step or two and review. A normal part of learning is forgetting. Heck, even big-brained primates go to school for a minimum of 12 years. Give your dog a break!

Raise the Criteria Once Each Step Is Learned

Let's go back to loose-leash walking as an example. Your dog is now looking at you while on leash. Take one step, click, and give a treat. Take another step, click, and treat. Continue to reinforce for each step for about five minutes. If the dog has been continually successful with one step, raise the criteria to two steps of loose-leash walking.

Your job is to advance behaviors, so don't get too stuck on each step when building a long behavior (such as loose-leash walking).

> **Pooch Pointers**
>
> If the behavior being taught is very complicated, an even shorter session is called for. Don't be afraid to train the dog for as little as 30 seconds or for just one correct repetition.

Keep Sessions Short and Successful

Continuous failure is a poor teacher. It can create a frustrated, aggressive, or quitter animal. The optimum sessions are three to five minutes in length, three to five times per day, working on only two to three behaviors each time.

Fix Bad Behaviors by Reinforcing Good Ones

Reinforce your dog for having four paws on the floor rather than jumping. Reinforce the dog for walking on a loose leash rather than pulling. Reinforce the dog for having a toy in his mouth rather than your arm. By focusing on the good stuff, the bad stuff usually goes away with very little extra training.

Watch Your Timing

Timing is everything. Improper timing using positive methods slows down learning. Improper timing using punishment methods constitutes abuse. Don't get me wrong—bad timing using positive methods can create more bad behaviors, but these are easy to fix once you fix your timing.

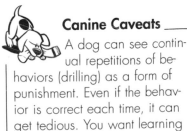

Canine Caveats

A dog can see continual repetitions of behaviors (drilling) as a form of punishment. Even if the behavior is correct each time, it can get tedious. You want learning to be fun for your dog, not something boring.

My rule of thumb: If the dog does something great, reinforce (or click and then reinforce if the dog is far away) within one-half second. If the dog does something less than desirable, wait for a full five to ten seconds after he stops doing the unwanted behavior, redirect to a better behavior, and then reinforce.

The Positives of Positive Training

Positive training is easy on the dogs, increases their love of learning (and of you), gives them a better quality of life, and overall helps them lead happier lives.

On the other hand, positive training is hard on the trainer (at first) because you have to learn to use your brain (ouch!). It is much easier to yell, scold, spank, hit, and generally get angry, than it is to think "What did *I* do to train my dog to act this way and what can I do to get him to stop?"

Thinking Is the Key

When our flawed human emotions come into play, our functioning brain cells disappear. It's hard to stop and reflect when we're emotionally charged. Once you're able to do that, however, training becomes easier and much more fun for you and your dog.

There's no magic answer to becoming more patient; it just takes practice and the sincere knowledge that losing your temper does nothing to help teach the dog anything. In fact, getting angry is more harmful than helpful.

Hand Saw Versus Band Saw: A Gentler Approach Is More Effective

Positive training is more effective for training any species, any behavior they're physically capable of doing. You might say, "But how can *not* punishing my dog actually be more effective? I *have* to tell him what he did wrong."

My motto is: If you aren't ignoring the dog (for "bad" behavior), then you're reinforcing it. We all love attention, and dogs are no exception. If we got attention only when we did "bad" things, then we'd do only "bad" things. If we were ignored when we did "bad" things, but reinforced when we did "good" things, then we would do only "good" things. (For the most part—don't forget, we are flawed human beings and we do make mistakes!)

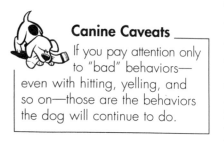

Canine Caveats

If you pay attention only to "bad" behaviors—even with hitting, yelling, and so on—those are the behaviors the dog will continue to do.

If you pay attention to only "good" behaviors, then your dog will continue to do those things that yield him your attention. If you pay attention to both "good" *and* "bad" behaviors, then you're confusing the heck out of your dog! Because both are being reinforced, the dog will continue to do both.

Or, at the very least, you're nagging and nagging the dog (saying "Sit, Sit, Sit" repeatedly, or not giving the dog any direction other than "NO!") until he just shuts you out completely. Think about when you're learning something new. How would you feel if every time you goofed, the teacher kept saying "wrong!" It would get really frustrating to say the least and you'd probably end up disliking the teacher or the subject.

Pooch Pointers

You can, in fact, "punish" your dog—and we positive trainers do punish our dogs, but not in the traditional sense of the word. We may withhold a reinforcer, or access to fun, or (horror of horrors) ignore the dog for a few seconds! Omigod! Call out the humane society!

The very idea that a dog "escapes punishment" or "gets away with it," is terrifying for some people. Our entire society is so based on punishment that it's hard for us to comprehend how an animal can actually learn better without it. But really, it works because as I mentioned before, attention is the best thing in the world to a dog (and humans, too). In fact, if you do physically or verbally punish the dog, you run a very high risk of creating much worse behaviors than the ones you started with.

Say that your teacher asks a question and you think you know the response. You raise your hand enthusiastically, blurt out your answer, and oops, you get it wrong. You get smacked for guessing incorrectly. The next time a question is asked you'll sit on your hands and avert your eyes to avoid the possibility of being called on. The rest of the class that witnessed your punishment will also be sitting on their hands.

Now for the flip side. The teacher walks in with a *huge* jar of candy and announces that anyone who attempts to answer a question will get a piece of candy. The students who give correct answers will get a whole *handful* of candy. More students will try harder, pay closer attention to the lesson, and do their homework more thoroughly and with more enjoyment. This system—positive reinforcement—encourages the students to *think!*

It's more effective to teach dogs' minds rather than manipulate their bodies. You should work with, rather than against, your dog during training sessions. And you should help inexperienced dogs rather than reprimand them.

Seattle Slew: Faster

Positively trained dogs—those that are not punished—will freely offer behaviors in an effort to elicit a good response from their trainers, will grasp information more quickly, and will be able to learn more advanced behaviors at a much earlier age than most other training methods allow.

> **Doggie Data**
>
> Leanne wanted to teach her dog Toby to lie down on his bed while Leanne was eating dinner, instead of mauling her and incessantly begging for food. In less than five minutes using the clicker and a small handful of treats, we taught Toby to go to his bed when Leanne was eating.

Behaviors that take months or years using punishment-based methods are now taking weeks, days, hours, or even minutes to teach using positive methods.

No Bad Side Effects

You may sometime hear the phrase "balanced training." There's nothing magical about balanced trainers, other than a nifty catch phrase.

What this means is that the trainer uses traditional, force-based techniques, as well as positive reinforcement when the dog is correct. For example, the trainer might pop up on the dog's neck with a prong collar for inattention and then reward him with a cookie for then looking at the trainer. As discussed previously, this is just confusing to the dog and makes him less likely to offer behaviors. This type of training teaches the dog to possibly work for you to avoid punishment, but it does not teach the dog to *willingly* work for you. Other dogs may just shut down from the punishment and end up doing absolutely nothing.

Punish your dog for "bad" behaviors and you risk creating aggression, fear, anxiety, *learned helplessness,* or a stubborn or stupid dog. Sure, you may immediately suppress the "bad" behavior, but that doesn't mean that the "bad" behavior is gone forever. For example:

Muttley Meanings

Learned helplessness occurs when the dog (or human) just shuts down because nothing he does is ever right, so he just gives up.

- 🏠 The dog might stop eating your socks, but he might start chewing on the wallpaper instead.

- 🏠 Punish your dog for jumping and he might become so afraid of people that he bites instead of jumping.

- 🏠 Punish your dog for doing a behavior wrong and he might become neurotic about trying again.

The true spirit of positive-based training is the trust the dog learns during the process. The trust that says he can offer behaviors without fear of recrimination. The trust that says, you will not hurt him. We owe it to our dogs to keep that trust.

The Least You Need to Know

- 🏠 The fundamentals of positive training include reinforcing good behavior, ignoring bad behavior, breaking down the desired behavior into small steps, and watching your timing.

- 🏠 Be sure you know what behaviors you want from your dog.

- 🏠 Redirect your dog, or better yet, stop "bad" behaviors before they start.

- 🏠 Positive training is better than negative training because it's easier, more effective, faster, has no bad side effects, and helps you and your dog have a happier relationship.

Eight Myths of Positive Training Dispelled

In This Chapter

- 🏠 Easy, fad-free training
- 🏠 Your dog always has a choice about how to behave
- 🏠 The tortoise or the hare—which is faster?
- 🏠 Dealing with barking and aggression the most effective way: positive training

Myths such as the ones that follow spring up out of nowhere, primarily because of the general lack of understanding of associative learning and operant conditioning. Here are my favorite responses to these misconceptions: It's hard to change our old habits and our old mindsets; however, you'll see that positive training isn't so difficult after all. Going against the "old school" may be difficult at times, but will be worth it in the end when you achieve a wonderful relationship with your dog.

Positive Training Is Not Just the Latest Craze and It Is Quite Easy to Learn

You're sure to hear discouraging comments such as these from your friends or other dog trainers: Positive and clicker training is a fad or gimmick, or the principles are too hard to learn and understand.

Myth #1: The Clicker Is a Fad or Gimmick

Actually, using a conditioned reinforcer (such as a clicker) is a training method based on sound, scientifically proven psychological principles, as discussed in Chapter 1. Skinner and others have conducted extensive research on the effectiveness of conditioned reinforcers in training.

As with anything, if you use the clicker or positive training improperly, it won't work. Put your car into neutral gear and it won't move forward when you step on the gas pedal. Give your dog a treat for barking, "to shut him up," and he'll continue to bark.

I've seen ill-informed trainers use the clicker as a recall signal, as a sound with no meaning (in other words, no treat follows the sound), or just randomly, with no thought of what they were actually reinforcing. Use it incorrectly and you can easily create aggression, fear, and avoidance.

Myth #2: The Principles Are Too Difficult to Learn and Understand

This is absolutely not true. Although positive training involves a lot of technical information, you don't have to be thoroughly versed, enmeshed, or overwhelmed to understand how it all works.

It's easy, however, to actually become a "behavior junkie" because learning how dogs learn is so fascinating. Many people come to me saying, "I just want a dog that doesn't jump or pull," and then become so mesmerized that they stay to learn more.

Canine Caveats

Without knowing the science behind the method, it's easy to fall back into the punishment mode of training, especially when we become frustrated by our dog's behavior.

The more you learn about the science of behavioral psychology, the more understanding and insight you gain and the better and more easily trained your dogs will be. Once you know the "whys" of behavior, it's then quite easy to fix problem behaviors—and better yet, stop them before they start.

Faster Learning That Enables the Dog to Make the *Right* Choices

Additional things you may hear from traditional-based trainers: Training using positive reinforcement/clickers takes much longer than traditional punishment-based training, and a dog should never be given a choice.

In this age of more things to do in less time, the word "faster" may be a real draw for us. However, when building a relationship, it takes as long as it takes. You can't rush a bond—with dogs or with other people. You certainly can't build that rapport using punishment.

We all make choices in our lives. Sometimes we choose incorrectly. That is called a mistake. Dogs and people trained using positive methods sometimes make the wrong choices, as do dogs and people trained using punishment methods. At times, we all make the wrong choices—humans and dogs—because none of us is perfect. Did you get beaten the last time you goofed? If your dog makes a mistake, lighten up!

Myth #3: Positive Reinforcement Takes Too Long

Actually, positive methods have been proven to speed up learning. In the beginning stages, it seems to take longer only because you may have to wait a whole five or ten (!) seconds for the dog to think, rather than forcing the dog into position.

However, once you and your dog catch on, clicker training leads to much faster results. (Dogs usually catch on faster than we humans do.) Dogs very quickly learn to perform the desired behaviors in order to make you click! In addition, behaviors learned through positive reinforcement and positive associations tend to stay with the dog for the rest of his life.

Try this "game" to see which takes longer, negative methods or positive methods. Get two friends to help you. One person will time both "trials." One person will be your subject.

1. Pick a simple behavior, such as opening a bag of potato chips and pouring the contents into a bowl. (Don't tell the subject what behavior you will "train" him or her to do.) Without any words at all from you, *lure* your friend into doing that behavior.

2. At each step of the way—picking up the bag, holding the bag at the edge, placing two hands on the bag, pulling the bag apart, and so on—if your subject makes a mistake, scream (and I mean scream loudly) "*No!*"

3. Resume luring the subject to complete the task. The timer stops when the task is complete. Be aware that your subject may get violent or simply quit the game. Your subject may also avoid direct eye contact with you and look at you only enough to complete the task. He or she may also laugh out of stress.

4. Then pick another behavior for the same person to accomplish— perhaps taking a light bulb out of a box and screwing it into a lamp.

5. Now, if at any time they get the steps wrong, instead of screaming *"No!"* you will say nothing, just stop luring, look away, count to three, and start again.

6. At each step, when they are correct, say a hearty, happy *"Yes!"* The timer stops when the task is accomplished.

Nine out of ten times, the behavior you trained using punishment will take twice as long as the behavior trained using positive feedback. Your subject may also tell you later how afraid he or she was while you were yelling and how much more pleasant it was when you were saying "yes." Your friend may also tell you that after the first behavior, he or she was still afraid to look at you, not fully trusting that you wouldn't start yelling again. You may also notice that after the "no" part, you were shaking like a leaf and needed to relax yourself.

Myth #4: In Training, a Dog Should Never Be Given a Choice

Clicker trainers set up the situation so that their dogs make the desired choices. Dogs always have behavioral choices, even when they're trained with aversives (corrections and/or punishment). To think they don't is an illusion.

I've seen dogs make mistakes regardless if they're trained using punishment *or* positive reinforcement. I've also seen people make mistakes—sometimes the same ones over and over again.

Let's Use Our Brains!

You may also hear: Positive/clicker training is too difficult because you must always have a clicker with you, and positively trained dogs won't work without food.

Many people think that once you start using a clicker, you must use one for the rest of your life—that you will have to surgically connect one to your hand. If you use the clicker properly, you will be using it in the beginning, teaching stages of each behavior, and then wean off of it.

There are still some trainers out there who believe that dogs should work because they love us and we should not have to bribe them with food. I believe that while there may be some dogs somewhere that do things because they "love" us, it's rare. Eventually, if you build a strong relationship with your dog, he may someday just want to work out of the sheer joy of doing things with you. I don't believe in bribing a dog—I believe in reinforcing a dog for correct behavior—a paycheck if you will. After all, most of us don't work for free unless we're independently wealthy.

Canine Caveats

Don't think that the relationship is included in the purchase price of a puppy—you have to earn that over the course of years. Dogs do things that work for them. Does that make them selfish? I don't think so. We all do things that work for us. That's what makes us human and what makes them dogs.

Myth #5: You Must Always Have the Clicker with You

Although most clicker trainers would probably admit to having clickers stashed everywhere (I personally found 15 clickers in my pocketbook the last time I cleaned it out), they're not necessary every time you work with your dog.

The clicker is used mostly when teaching a new behavior in the beginning stages. You can phase it out once the behavior is well learned. Thus, it is very important to make sure certain words become secondary reinforcers. I use the words "yes," and "that's right" as my "click words." Sometimes it just isn't logical or practical to be holding food, clicker, toys, and the leash to use as reinforcers. Use these words not as praise, but as a marker signal followed by a reward, just as you would reward after a click.

Myth #6: Clicker-Trained Dogs Won't Work Without Food

I could counter that with saying that punishment-trained dogs won't work without punishment. In the beginning stages of training, I recommend that you use food liberally. Many times, the dogs have no real positive connection with their owners and food helps to jump-start that connection.

However, a good positive/clicker trainer learns how to go from *continuous* to *variable schedules of reinforcement* and to use other types of reinforcers. Punishment-based trainers often say to me, "Well, you can't bring a clicker into the obedience ring." My reply is, "Well, you can't bring a prong or shock collar into the ring, either."

Food is easier sometimes to deliver and doesn't take much thought—get a behavior right, get a cookie. But if you use *only* food as reinforcement, the naysayers will be right—your dog will work only for food. Using other types of reinforcers, such as petting, play, or silly games, takes more thought and planning, but the benefits are enormous (see Chapter 9).

 Muttley Meanings

If you give your dog a treat each and every time he does a correct behavior, you're following a **continuous schedule of reinforcement**. If sometimes you give the dog a treat for a correct behavior and sometimes you don't, you're following a **variable schedule of reinforcement**.

 Doggie Data

Jan was trying to teach Carrie, her Portuguese Water Dog, to (on land) take a water float, run 15 feet past a marker buoy, and drop it when Jan said "drop." Carrie was taking the float nicely but wasn't going past the buoy far enough or fast enough and was continually looking back to Jan.

Up to this point, Jan had been using only food for reinforcers. She went on a more variable schedule of reinforcement with variable types of reinforcements, such as petting, praise, and toys. Within four repetitions, Carrie was going out faster and farther.

Like the Dependable Maytag Repair Man

Many people believe that behaviors taught using positive methods aren't as reliable as behaviors taught using force. And even with evidence to the contrary, there are still some trainers who don't believe that positive training can work for behavior problems like barking or aggression.

Positive is the only correct and effective way to work with aggression. Answer aggression with aggression and what do you get? More aggression! If you say to your dog, "I'll beat you, shock you, and punish you until you like this person (or dog)," then you might as well cash it in now. Reliability in training is all about taking small steps in training and setting the dog up to be right.

Myth #7: Force Works Better

Although a dog's desire to avoid pain is strong, the desire to gain pleasant consequences is stronger. Think about the last time you got a speeding ticket—did it stop you from speeding? Much of your dog's behavior is based on what's more reinforcing for him do to.

Let's say you're stopped by the police each time you're not speeding and are rewarded with $100. Every day for a week, you're stopped two or three times per day and handed $100. Then the police go to a random schedule of reinforcement. Now you get stopped only one or two times per day and only three or five times per week. Sometimes you get verbally praised, sometimes you're handed dinner tickets to your favorite restaurant, and sometimes you get the $100.

Pooch Pointers

Reliability is the bane of all dog trainers, whether or not you compete in the show ring. None of us is 100 percent reliable in everything, and neither are our dogs. Use your head when needed. Don't let your dog off the leash to run rampant in the neighborhood and expect him to come when called.

Once in a while you get pulled over and handed $1,000. Would you ever speed again? I sure wouldn't. I would take that money and run out and buy a van with cruise control because I wouldn't want to miss the chance of possibly getting the rewards! In the same respect, once a dog has learned something (good or bad), he tends to repeat that behavior over and over. Behaviors learned through force tend to fall apart when the dog is under stress. But behaviors learned in pleasant circumstances with positive consequences are less likely to fall apart under pressure.

Myth #8: Positive Training Isn't Effective with Barking or Aggression

Dogs trained using a clicker can be easily taught alternate behaviors to replace the unwanted ones. Trainers using positive principles often devise very creative ways to change undesirable behaviors such as barking and aggression. I've personally used a clicker to solve a number of serious behavioral and aggression problems.

I've seen dogs barking in crates. I've seen their owners come up to the crate, kick it, yell at the dog, take the dog out of the crate when they can't stand it anymore or if it becomes an embarrassment, and otherwise reinforce the dog for barking in the crate.

Canine Caveats

Positive is the *only* way to reliably reduce or eliminate aggression. Just ask any marine mammal trainer!

I've seen owners put collars on their dogs that deliver an electric shock or a spray of citronella to get them to stop barking. After a few zaps with the shock collar or some sprays with the citronella collar, they hang the collar on the crate and say, "See? The dog is now not barking." True, but take the collar away and the dog starts barking again because now the threat of punishment is no longer there. And the dog hasn't learned anything constructive, such as being quiet in the crate.

Doggie Data _____

Rudy, a four-month-old Rottweiler, had been attacked by his veterinarian—yes, veterinarian! Rudy had gone in for his puppy shots, was nervous in this new situation, and growled while backing away. The veterinarian then grabbed Rudy by the neck, threw him to the ground in an "alpha roll," and then held him up in the air and shook him (known as a "scruff shake") because "that's how you _have_ to treat Rottweilers."

As a result, Rudy became aggressive toward humans. He was terrified of anyone other than his family, and especially hated touching or people approaching. I worked with Rudy for a series of classes. Now he runs up to people for petting and treats and is back to being the happy puppy he used to be.

Aggression can be easily (although not necessarily quickly) corrected by using positive methods. You can't answer aggression with aggression and expect the dog to become friendly. The effects of punishment are explained more thoroughly in Chapter 4.

Canine Caveats _____

Two methods used in traditional training to show a dog who's boss are alpha rolls and scruff shakes. Grappling the dog to the ground and holding him in a submissive position is called an alpha roll. Grabbing the dog by the side of the neck, holding him off the ground, and yelling at him is called a scruff shake.

Please, pretty please, stay away from doing these! They will only frighten your dog and end up making him aggressive.

The Least You Need to Know

- 🏠 Positive training is based on proven scientific principles; it's not a fad, and it's easy to learn.

- 🏠 Punishment training takes longer than positive training.

- 🏠 Dogs always have choices in how they behave, regardless of the consequences and the training method.

- 🏠 Positive training is the only reliable way to deal with aggression and barking.

Chapter  4

Side Effects of Punishment

In This Chapter

- 🏠 Causes of bad behavior and the effects of punishment
- 🏠 *High Anxiety* and the *Fear Factor*
- 🏠 Does your dog ignore you? Uh-oh …
- 🏠 Keep up your liability insurance: aggressive dogs
- 🏠 Beyond punishment: learned helplessness

Punishment can create so many toxic side effects, I'd be afraid to use it. That doesn't mean that sometimes I'm not tempted—I'm human after all, and at times my dogs annoy the heck out of me. But I never resort to it. Increased use of punishment does not stop "bad" behaviors. They just get worse.

The Negative Spiral of Punishment

Some dogs may tolerate more punishment than others. Some of them are happy, willing workers—or seem to be. After a while however, they may shut down and refuse to work or develop neurotic behaviors that seemingly came out of nowhere.

What Is Punishment?

So what constitutes punishment to a dog? The sky's the limit here—verbal reprimands, yelling, screaming, hitting, spanking, slapping, leash jerks, shock collars, head halters, choke collars, hoses, spray bottles, soda cans with pennies in them, citronella collars—anything that's meant to stop behaviors in a negative way.

A mommy dog may grab a puppy dog by the neck and reprimand the pup. What we as humans fail to see are the "okay, okay, I'll stop" signs that the puppy gives. Mommy dog does see these signs and relents immediately. Humans are simply incapable of detecting those signs because we are not dogs.

If we try to do this to a dog and the dog says "uncle," we have no clue and continue on. What can this cause? The pup will now get really angry because he has been trying to say he is "sorry" and yet you continue to pound him. He may then bite, growl, or become afraid of you.

Now you have trained your puppy that even if he submits, he is going to be punished anyway. This will lead to an aggressive, fearful dog or one that goes into learned helplessness because he is not able to get the punishment to stop.

Escalating Punishment

Say your dog pulls on the leash. The first time, you yank him back. The next time, you yell at him. The third time, you hit him. Now you put a prong collar on him and continue to hit, yell, scream, and yank back. He is still pulling on the leash. And now, because of the punishment, he's possibly aggressing at people or dogs.

Your dog jumps on people coming to the door. Today you push him down. He comes back for more. You push him down harder. Up he goes again. You knee him in the chest. He finally stops jumping. You are positively reinforced for using punishment because, "see it worked!" The next time he jumps, you will knee him in the chest.

Tomorrow he is jumping again. You start with kneeing him in the chest—because "it worked yesterday." It isn't working today, so you squeeze his paws so tightly that he screams in pain. He stops jumping—today. *You* are reinforced again for using punishment: "Okay, *now* I get it—I have to squeeze his paws until he screams." And what will you do tomorrow?

Observable Effects of Punishment

We can't assume (because we all know what happens when we assume) that we know how an animal is feeling or what he's thinking, but we can observe and measure behaviors. Punish your dog and these six behaviors *will happen in this order*, and they can be reliably observed and measured:

- **Anxiety**   Measurable by body chemistry
- **Fear**   Observable behavior
- **Escape**   Observable behavior
- **Avoidance**   Observable behavior
- **Aggression**   Observable behavior
- **Learned helplessness**   Observable behavior

Causes of "Bad" Behaviors

There are many causes of "bad" behaviors, most of which we can alleviate. The top three sources of these reactions are the following:

- Punishment from humans
- Punishment from other animals
- Punishment from the environment

Additional stimuli that can create different levels of arousal include thunder, grooming, vet visits, people, other dogs, other animals,

40 **Part 1:** Positively Amazing: What Is Positive Training and Why Should I Use It?

cars, bikes, kids, being left alone, large groups, buildings, petting, toenail clipping, being on leash, men, hats, umbrellas, grass, concrete, gravel, linoleum, balloons … you name it, there's a dog out there afraid of it.

What is the root of these problems? It can be many things including improper socialization, or none at all. A fearful mother (dog) can pass along her neurosis. And the *biggie:* punishment from us for reacting out of nervousness or fear.

You may do one of two things when your dog shows signs of fear:

🐾 Try to soothe and pet the dog: "It's okay Rover, Uncle Bob won't bite you."

🐾 Yell and smack the dog: "Don't you *dare* growl at Aunt Helen!"

Either way you respond is reinforcing the dog for the behavior you don't want. If you try to comfort the dog, the dog is reinforced for the fearful or aggressive behaviors. If you punish the dog, still thinking that you have to show the dog when he's wrong, you're creating the wrong association—he then learns that bad things happen around that stimulus (be it a person or dog or whatever). Since the dog is already in stress mode, where he's unable to think at all, you have just added even more stress and pain. The next time he encounters that particular stimulus, his negative reaction will intensify and escalate faster.

Very often it's our reactions or punishment that create worse problems than what we started with. What may have started out as mild anxiety can quickly grow into full-blown aggression.

Pooch Pointers

What we humans may perceive as benign may be perceived by each individual dog as being horrible. It's not up to us to decide for our dogs, or anyone else for that matter, what's scary or not scary. I love thunderstorms, yet one of my friends is so afraid of them, she hides in the closet and cries.

Doggie Data _____

Faith brought her Flat-Coated Retriever, Carmen, to me because he continually ran out of the ring during agility competition. Carmen was also exhibiting "deafness" (avoidance) and showed a complete disregard to Faith's presence.

Faith came from a background of using punishment to train her dogs. Although it was hard for her to change her thinking at first, she knew she had to do something to change her dog's behavior. As a result of positive training, Carmen now comes when called, even amidst distractions, responds to cues the first time (not the fiftieth time), allows handling, walks on a loose leash, and even does a great imitation of competition heeling. He's better mannered at home and very attentive to Faith.

Lions and Tigers and Bears, Oh My! Anxiety and Fear

What's happening after you punish the dog either verbally or physically? He becomes anxious and tries to appease and diffuse your anger with submissive doggie gestures. Some of the signs of a dog's anxiety that we humans incorrectly perceive as "looking guilty" may be a lowered head, tail tucked between legs, ears back, and even a submissive grin. We assume (there's that word again) that the dog "knows what he did wrong."

The observable signs of anxiety can also include the following:

🏠 Nervousness

🏠 Pacing

🏠 Whining

🏠 Drooling

🏠 Sniffing

🏠 Yawning

🏠 Barking

- 🏠 Chewing

- 🏠 Obsessive licking (licking feet or body parts compulsively as to cause sores)

- 🏠 Inattention to owner and many of the signals listed in Chapter 7

Doggie Data _____

A woman called me to ask about housetraining. It turns out her dog runs away from her when she tries to approach. When I asked her what she was doing, she said she was hitting the dog for soiling the house. I explained that punishment is not the proper or effective way to housetrain a dog. Her response: "Oh, I don't punish my dog, I only hit her."

Think about it from your own perspective: You have a boss who's very punishing—nothing you ever do is right. You go to work each day with a heavy heart and dragging feet. You start to develop physical or emotional symptoms related to anxiety disorders. You may still be able to function, but you'll be sure to do the absolute minimum required, cut corners, and shirk responsibility wherever possible.

To think that our dogs will suffer no side effects when we punish them is just downright unreasonable. Of course there are side effects! If there were no effects of punishment, then "anxiety disorder" wouldn't be in the dictionary!

Fear is another consequence of using punishment. Some of the signs of fear can be the following:

- 🏠 Hiding

- 🏠 Hackles up

- 🏠 Wide eyes

- 🏠 Growling

- 🏠 Backing away

- 🏠 Evacuation of bowels

- 🏠 Shaking

Say your friend comes to the house and your (as yet untrained) dog jumps on her. Your friend then knees your dog in the chest in an attempt to get the dog to stop jumping. Your dog then hides behind the toilet in fear for the rest of that person's stay.

Your dog is perfectly justified in feeling afraid. He acted in a normal doggie manner—this is how dogs greet each other. Since you haven't (yet) trained him to do any alternate behaviors (like lie down when someone approaches), he's stunned and frightened when this horrible beast of a person *hurts* him for greeting the person in the only way he knows how.

The next time your friend comes to visit, your dog becomes anxious and may take one look and growl, back away, or evacuate his bowels. This may look like aggression to you, but it is fear, and for good reason. Pain was inflicted on him the last time he saw that person.

Doggie Data _____

Your dog soils the house in your absence. You come home and yell at the dog. Of course, he has no clue why you're punishing him. So he learns that "homecoming" is a stressful and fearful time.

Maybe you're from the school of thought that advocates "don't punish unless you catch him in the act." If so, you then lay in wait for him to soil the house and then whammo! You punish the dog. What has the dog learned then? To be afraid of you and to run and hide and soil behind the couch where you can't see him because eliminating around you is dangerous.

Punishment doesn't teach the dog anything constructive and it can actually backfire because dogs don't make the same associations that we do. Why? Because dogs are dogs and not fuzzy children. Punishment can in fact suppress behaviors that *will* come out in other neurotic and inappropriate ways.

I'm Not Deaf—I'm Ignoring You: Escape and Avoidance

Next up on the countdown of behaviors caused by punishment are escape and avoidance. They're actually quite similar—it all depends on how the dog manifests them.

Escape can include the following:

- Running away

- Digging out of the yard or kennel

- Scratching at doors

- Hiding under or behind furniture

- Slipping out of collars

If your dog would rather be lost in the woods, eat bark from trees, sleep out in the raw elements without any of the creature comforts such as air-conditioning, heat, running water, three square meals per day, and a soft bed, then you may want to reexamine your relationship with your dog.

If, at the slightest opportunity, your dog flies out of the door ("I'm outta here!"), what do you think may be the problem? The correct answer should *not* have in it this statement: "My dog is a (fill in the breed here), so of course he runs away." Breed has nothing to do with a dog's running away—chances are you're using punishment to train your dog and he wants to get away from it.

Avoidance is the second half of this equation. There are two kinds of avoidance: passive avoidance and active avoidance. Passive avoidance includes the following:

- Ignoring

- Avoiding eye contact or petting

- "Selective deafness"

Active avoidance includes the following:

🐾 Not coming when called

🐾 Staying out of reach

🐾 Inattention to owner

Avoidance, whether it's active or passive, is probably one of the most widely used reactions to punishment. Dogs do it, humans do it, and maybe even the birds and bees do it. For those of us (and I include dogs in that list) who hate confrontation, avoidance is the way to go. Dogs have all sorts of rituals linked to avoiding conflict. The calming signals dogs send to each other are all about avoiding aggression and "arguments."

As the punishment in their lives increases, escape and avoidance behaviors are the last maneuvers dogs use before aggression starts. This is the last level you can attain using punishment before your problems really shoot through the roof. Start positive training *now* to regain your dog's trust.

Doggie Data

Dora came to me with her dog Stanley who was developing some aggression problems that she was concerned about. He was acting as if Dora was invisible and that he was deaf. After only a few lessons with positive training, Stanley regained his hearing, and his attention to Dora is astounding. Once she has completed his desensitization program, Dora plans on resuming Stanley's show career.

Canine Caveats

I mean it. If your dog is displaying the early warning signs of anxiety, fear, escape, and avoidance, *do not* wait any longer to fix these using positive methods. If you increase your punishment to try to correct the problem, you may as well cash it in now. Be sure your insurance is paid up because this dog will become a danger to you and others.

Meltdown: Aggression

Aggression is a learned behavior. That's hard to comprehend sometimes, and we may want to try to justify and explain away the

46 **Part 1:** Positively Amazing: What Is Positive Training and Why Should I Use It?

aggression by saying, "Well, what do you expect from a (insert name of breed here)." That only gets rid of any guilt or denial you may feel, but it doesn't help you get out of the problem that punishment caused.

The breed of dog has nothing to do with aggression. Yes, this includes even the breeds that have so recently made headlines for mauling people. Bad training methods are bad training methods. Period. Answer aggression with aggression and think you'll get a happy, well-adjusted dog? Think again, baby! I've worked with many of the so-called "aggressive" breeds and found them to be wonderfully smart, sweet, and teachable.

Signs of Aggression

Some of the more obvious signs of aggression are the following:

- 🏠 Growling
- 🏠 Biting
- 🏠 Snarling
- 🏠 Snapping
- 🏠 Attacking

When I come across a dog that growls at me, I get down and kiss his feet (well, not literally) and thank him for warning me. Punish the dog for giving off a warning and guess what? You won't get warnings anymore—you'll just get a bite.

Types and Causes of Aggression

There are many, many causes of aggression, and most of them, if not all, can be corrected. For example, some people who own aggressive dogs may deliberately encourage the dog because they enjoy the feeling of power or of feeling protected.

The short list of causes:

1. Territoriality

2. Putting animals in a position to feel vulnerable to attack by other dogs (such as forcing their heads away by the use of head halters)

3. Influx of new members to the household (canine or human)

Canine Caveats

Neutering doesn't get rid of aggression, because aggression is a learned behavior. There's no "aggressive gene" in testicles. This doesn't mean that I don't agree with neutering—I whole-heartedly do, but not as the "cure" for aggression.

4. Resource guarding—can be food, objects, or humans

5. Hormonal—normal seasonal fluctuations, such as breeding, arousal level, or cycling females

6. Physical stress—injury, illness, drugs, reactions to collars or corrections

7. Responses to punishment

8. *Scheduled induced aggression*—incorrect use of a reinforcement schedule

9. Our responses to aggression—accidental reinforcement

10. Observational learning—allowing dogs to chase or attack other animals

 Muttley Meanings

Scheduled induced aggression is angry behavior that results when the results you get don't match your expectations. You know that if you put money in a soda machine, your purchase comes out. If you put money in and nothing comes out, what do you do? You may kick the machine, pound on it, rock it, or grab a sledgehammer and pound it. Why? Because we've learned that putting money into the machine *always* yields us a soda. When it doesn't, we get mad.

Correcting Aggression

The first step in controlling and preventing aggression is understanding the situations that frequently trigger the aggressive responses in your dog. Once you're aware, don't let your dog practice that behavior by repeatedly putting him in that situation.

Although punishment (from humans) may initially *suppress* aggressive behaviors, dogs learn to mask the early observable (to humans) aggressive signals in order to avoid punishment. Punishment can actually lead to and cause a variety of negative manifestations, including aggression.

Doggie Data _____

Buddy lived in a household with three other dogs. When a fifth dog was brought in, Buddy did an about-face in behavior. Even though he used to be a "doggie diplomat"—very gentle and nice to strange dogs—he became very fearful and would growl and snap at other dogs.

What happened? It turns out, the fifth dog was very punishing to Buddy and Buddy was showing redirected aggression to other dogs. Once the fifth dog was managed better and the punishing stopped, Buddy went back to being his normal, sweet self.

And was the fifth dog punished? No way! He was heavily reinforced for presenting friendly behavior and soon stopped bullying Buddy on his own!

Remember when I said aggression is a learned behavior? Aggression, from the dog's point of view, keeps the animal safe from danger. If a scary thing appears out of nowhere and startles the dog, the dog aggresses, and the scary thing either goes away or the owner takes the dog away. The aggressive behavior worked and will be repeated the next time the dog is afraid.

(Photo by P. Dennison)

Dogs being frustrated by a barrier and aggressing.

Learned Helplessness

Increase your punishment so much so that the dog no longer has any other recourse or alternatives to protect himself and you'll create learned helplessness (think of it as doggie depression). Some of the signs are the following:

- 🏠 Cowering
- 🏠 Rolling over
- 🏠 Submission
- 🏠 Eyes glazed over
- 🏠 Motionless (can be frozen in a submissive posture)
- 🏠 Appearing catatonic or deaf

Behavioral science shows us that continual use of inescapable punishment teaches the dog to do literally nothing—to be helpless. As the punishment escalates, the level of intensity of the dog's reactions will increase from anxiety right up to learned helplessness. If the intensity of the punishment is so high with no escape possible, *all* mammals will go into learned helplessness.

Efforts to prod him into action will most likely be ineffectual. Even when presented with further punishment, the dog will do nothing further to avoid the punishment and just endure quietly whatever additional castigation you dole out.

I hope I have convinced you to cease and desist any and all punishments. I don't care what behavior problem you have, punishment is *never* warranted.

The Least You Need to Know

- Causes of "bad" behaviors can include punishment from humans, other dogs, and the environment.

- If you aren't ignoring "bad" behavior, you *are* reinforcing it.

- Punishment only makes us feel better; it does nothing to stop "bad" behaviors.

- Punishment creates more problems, such as anxiety, fear, escape, avoidance, aggression, and learned helplessness.

Part  Lassie In the Classroom: How Dogs Learn and Communicate

Continuing on our incredible journey, here's where you find out how dogs learn, how to positively fix mistakes and even stop them from happening in the first place, and how to understand what your dog is telling you. Dogs do have a language all their own (and it isn't English). We can learn to read them and speak to them, and use our knowledge to train them and keep them safe and happy.

After reading Part 1, you might see some mistakes that you've already made with your dog—not to worry. Dogs are amazingly adaptable and resilient, so you can fix these problems with positive methods. You'll learn how to maximize "life rewards" to get the most out of your dog's training.

Chapter 5

Learning Their ABCs

In This Chapter

- 🏠 The ABCs of learning
- 🏠 Math revisited: negative, positive, reinforcement, punishment
- 🏠 Good and bad associations
- 🏠 Associative learning and operant conditioning are always happening

As I touched on a little in Chapter 1, the basis of all learning (for both humans and dogs) happens within either associative learning or operant conditioning.

The definition of learning is "a change in behavior due to experience." Most certainly, as positive trainers, we want those experiences to be pleasant ones. We all know that behavior is influenced by its consequences. We reward or punish people and dogs so that they will behave in different ways.

The Basis of All Learning

There are three components to every *learned* behavior. Just remember your ABCs:

🏠 **Antecedent**   A cue, or something that comes before a behavior

🏠 **Behavior**   What the animal does, resulting from the cue

🏠 **Consequence**   What happens directly after the behavior

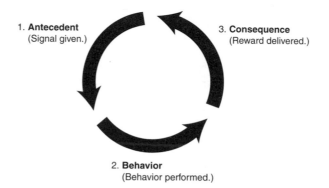

1. **Antecedent**
(Signal given.)

3. **Consequence**
(Reward delivered.)

2. **Behavior**
(Behavior performed.)

The sequence in which operant conditioning happens. You can't have the behavior before the antecedent, and you can't have the consequence before the behavior.

Doggie Data

Edward Thorndike, a well-known behaviorist, studied consequences of behavior in numerous experiments. In one of his experiments, a cat was enclosed in a box. As the cat struggled to escape, she accidentally moved the latch that opened the door. When she was enclosed in the box a few more times, the cat would start to press the latch right away. The behavior of releasing the latch increased because the consequence of getting out of the box was rewarding. (There was food outside of the box.)

A Is for Antecedent

An antecedent, more commonly called a "cue" (but then it would be CBC rather than ABC), is anything that happens *before* a behavior.

We're surrounded daily by all different kinds of antecedents and adjust our behavior accordingly. For a person, this can be the red traffic light, a lightning bolt, the alarm clock, the promise of a paycheck, Mom saying "let's all go for ice cream," or the doorbell ringing. To a dog, antecedents can include a person approaching, the can opener, or seeing the leash coming out. These are all antecedents that tell a person or dog how to react next.

B Is for Behavior

The next step in your ABCs is "B," the behavior—or how you or your dog will respond to the antecedent. The red light tells you to stop, the lightning bolt tells you to run for cover, the alarm clock wakes you up, the promise of a paycheck inspires you to work, "Ice cream" is pretty obvious, and a doorbell ringing means answer the door. To a dog, a person approaching means jump up and display submissive behavior, like licking and pawing at the person (unless you've trained him that a person approaching is a cue to sit). Hearing the can opener means run to the kitchen, and seeing the leash coming out of the closet means run to the door.

(Photo by P. Dennison)

A dog that has been taught to understand that a person approaching is a cue to sit.

C Is for Consequence

So what happens once you've seen the antecedent and done the behavior? Now comes the "C," the consequence. Stop at a red light and you won't get into an accident or get a ticket. Run for cover and you won't get struck by lightning. Wake up when the alarm rings and you won't be late for work. Pick up your paycheck and you get to go shopping and pay your bills. Again, the ice cream is obvious.

Pooch Pointers

Every event in our daily lives has an antecedent, behavior, and consequence. The antecedent can be a sign of something pleasant or something punishing.

Canine Caveats

Please don't allow a puppy to do what you won't want him to do as an adult dog. It will only confuse and stress the dog, and annoy the heck out of you.

You open the door, Publisher's Clearing House is there, and you've won a million dollars (and now you don't have to set the alarm anymore to get up and go to work).

The dog gets attention for jumping (or for sitting), he gets fed after the can is opened, and he goes for a walk after the leash is put on.

The behavior and consequence can also be something good or bad and can change. For instance, if you allow your puppy to bite you when you're playing with him, here's how you've trained your dog:

🏠 You get down on the floor (antecedent).

🏠 The dog bites you for attention (behavior).

🏠 You play with the dog to get him to stop biting you (consequence).

Now the dog is older and you no longer want him to bite you, so here's what you can do:

🏠 You get down on the floor (antecedent).

🏠 The dog bites you with adult teeth and it hurts (behavior).

🏠 You punish the dog by hitting or yelling at him, or you use the proper positive trainer response, which is get up and leave (consequence).

With Four, You Get Egg Roll: The Main Principles of Operant Conditioning

Positive reinforcement, negative reinforcement, positive punishment, and negative punishment are the main terms of operant conditioning, and these can get very confusing at first.

In science, the terms "positive" and "negative" relate only to adding something or taking something away. The terms "reinforcement" and "punishment" relate to behavior increasing or decreasing:

🏠 **Positive Reinforcement (+R)**   Anything *good* that is *added* (positive) that *increases* (reinforces) behavior.

🏠 **Positive Punishment (+P)**   Anything *bad* that is *added* (positive) that *decreases* (punishes) behavior.

🏠 **Negative Reinforcement (–R)**   Anything *bad* that is *taken away* (negative) to *increase* (reinforce) behavior.

🏠 **Negative Punishment (–P)**   Anything *good* that is *taken away* (negative) to *decrease* (punishes) behavior.

Now that you're thoroughly confused, the following sections give you some examples to help you gain a better understanding of these concepts.

Positive Reinforcement

Here are some examples: Your dog sits when you ask him to and you give him a treat; his sitting behavior will increase in the future.

Pooch Pointers

Positive reinforcement establishes "good" behaviors faster and creates a love of learning and a great relationship. Positive reinforcement doesn't create confusion and stress or any bad behaviors—unless you reinforce "bad" behaviors.

You give your dog treats for walking on a loose leash, and his loose-leash-walking behavior will increase. You reinforce your dog for not re-arranging the furniture, and "lying down calmly" behaviors will increase. You reinforce your dog for having "four on the floor," and his staying on the floor behavior will increase.

Positive Punishment

Don't be confused by this—positive means something added, not necessarily something nice. Your dog is barking and you turn on the citronella collar. His barking may decrease. Your dog urinates on the rug and you hit him with a newspaper, and his eliminating on the rug behavior may decrease. You touch a hot stove and burn your hand. You will not touch a hot stove again.

Please don't get the wrong idea here—I am *not* advocating positive punishment. In fact, I highly recommend you stay away from it. There are too many toxic side effects. The timing has to be perfect (if you punish the dog for soiling the house after he comes to you, you have just punished him for coming to you), and punishment is associated with the person doling it out.

Canine Caveats

You really can't get rid of Pavlov. You positively punish your dog by shocking him with an electric shock collar when he barks in his crate to stop the barking. He now has the association that being in his crate is a very horrible thing.

Oftentimes, you only suppress behavior using positive punishment—sure, the dog stops urinating on the carpet, but now does it behind the couch. For some dogs, barking is so self-reinforcing (they like to bark) that they'll bark regardless of what you do, or bark only when the shock or citronella collar is off. The punishment has to outweigh the rewards and the motivation for it to be effective.

Depending on the motivation, some people (and dogs) will go to great lengths to succeed over adversity, continuing to practice their success-seeking behaviors regardless of punishment or hardships.

Negative Reinforcement

Negative reinforcement increases a behavior by taking something away that the dog doesn't like. Of course, you must have already added these punishers to be able to then take them away.

So what starts out as positive punishment can end up being negative reinforcement. The choke collar is yanked and then loosened up when the dog stops pulling. You hit the dog and then stop hitting him when he ceases to jump. The electricity is turned off and then turned back on after you pay the bill.

As with positive punishment—don't do it!

Doggie Data

Historically, we humans are controlled primarily through negative reinforcement. We're punished when we haven't done what is reinforcing to those that are in "charge" (such as parents, employers, or trainers). Positive reinforcement has, unfortunately, been less often used, but it is more effective than negative reinforcement and has many fewer unwanted by-products.

For example, a student is punished when he doesn't study. He may study after that, but he may also stay away from school (truancy), vandalize school property, attack teachers, or do nothing. With positive reinforcement, the student would have been reinforced for studying in the first place, and most likely would have learned to love learning.

Negative Punishment

This sounds like the most awful option, doesn't it? It isn't, though, and in fact is the method of choice that positive trainers use to punish their dogs. I did tell you that I do punish my dogs and this is how I do it.

Negative punishment reduces behaviors by taking away or withholding something good or something the dog will work for. Your dog jumps on you and you walk away, thus withholding the attention he craves. His jumping behavior will decrease.

Your dog is being pushy and demanding attention. You walk away, denying the dog your attention. The next time your dog will sit politely for attention, reducing the pushy behavior. You ask your dog to sit and he looks at you blankly. You withhold the treat. The next time you ask him to sit, he will sit, reducing the "looking at you blankly" behavior.

You're playing ball with your dog and he brings it back but won't drop it. You end the game. The next time you play ball, he will drop the ball, reducing the "hold onto the ball at all costs" behavior. The bad do bad because the bad is rewarded. The good do good because the good is rewarded.

Ring a Bell? Associative Learning

Associative learning is an association between two *stimuli*. Of these two stimuli, one is neutral and in the beginning has no meaning. The other stimulus is one that does already have meaning for the dog (or human). The stimulus can be pleasant, or it can be unpleasant.

 Muttley Meanings
Stimuli (the plural of stimulus) are any events that affect or are capable of affecting behavior.

The two main events that humans or dogs don't need to learn to react to without training are food and pain. Almost everything else is a learned association.

Let's go back (just for a minute) to Pavlov and the metronome and the dog and the saliva. When Pavlov first started pairing the sound of the metronome just before food was presented, the dogs did not drool. However, over time, with consistent pairing (metronome and then food), the dogs began to salivate at the sound of the metronome. As far as their automatic reactions were concerned, the metronome meant food.

Canine Caveats

Why is the *order* in which things are associated important? Because if you say "Sit" while the dog is standing and continue to say "Sit," then the dog will learn that "Sit" means to stand. If you want your dog to sit when you say "Sit," then pair the word *with the action of sitting.*

Why Is Associative Learning Used?

Associative learning is used for two reasons:

🏠 To create an association between a stimulus that would not normally have any meaning along with a stimulus that would have meaning

🏠 To train automatic responses (like drooling)

The recess bell has no meaning until it's paired with playtime; the word "Sit" has no meaning unless paired with sitting; and the smoke alarm has no meaning until you see the fire.

Let's say you hear a song you've never heard before, playing on the radio at the dentist's office while you're getting a particularly painful root canal. The next time you hear that song, you may switch radio stations; in fact, you may never listen to that radio station again. Next you hear a different song when you meet "your true love." Whenever you hear this song, loving, misty feelings come over you.

Your dog meets a person who gives him lots of yummy treats. The next time he meets that person, he'll be happy to see her (and probably salivate!). Associations, especially first ones, are vitally important to how a dog views his world. You can easily create a happy, well-adjusted dog or a fearful, aggressive dog by the associations you allow him to have.

Hobnobbing with the Wrong Crowd: Bad Associations

Setting up a dog to be fearful or aggressive is quite easy to do. Here's how: Make sure all his associations are bad ones. For example, let your dog meet someone who will knee him in the chest or yell if he jumps. The next time he meets that person, your dog won't be happy to see him or her. Do this enough times and your dog will be fearful of people.

Here are some other ways to set up bad associations: Introduce your young puppy to an older dog who isn't good around puppies and watch your dog grow fearful or aggressive toward strange dogs. Yell at your dog for myriad "bad" behaviors and he'll learn to either ignore you or be afraid of you. Call your dog to come and then punish him for something he did an hour ago, and the word "Come" will now take on a negative connotation. Hit your dog for growling at a child and watch your dog learn to hate children (and probably progress from growling to biting). Punish your dog for making a mistake during training and he will then associate training with pain, which certainly does nothing to help him love learning.

Canine Caveats

Beware of "negative" associative learning. Your dog runs away and comes back an hour later. You punish him for running away. The next time you say "Come," he will stay away because that word was paired with unpleasant things.

Keep Those Good Associations Happenin'

So what *can* you do? Make sure the associations are good ones! Have your puppy play with friendly dogs and meet nice, dog-friendly people. Use positive reinforcement as your training philosophy. Get rid of punishments from people, dogs, and (as much as possible) the environment.

Whenever you run across something potentially scary that you want your dog not to be neurotic about, just add some positive stimuli and it will turn out alright. Let's say your dog is afraid of other dogs barking. The next time you hear a dog barking, start feeding the heck out of your dog, before he becomes afraid. If your dog is afraid of people approaching, pair food with a person approaching.

Pooch Pointers

Yes, even the environment can be punishing. Inanimate objects can be dangerous! Lamps can fall, baby gates can get stuck on doggies' necks, doors can slam in faces, and paws can get stuck in crate doors. Honking horns and wailing sirens can send many a dog under the table in fear.

Use associations properly and just be cognizant that Pavlov is always sitting on your shoulder—24 hours a day, 7 days a week. Become Ronald McDonald, Bozo the Clown, and Howdy Doody all rolled up in one. It's a jungle out there—don't become one of the "bad guys."

The Least You Need to Know

- All learned behaviors have an antecedent, a behavior, and a consequence.

- Positive reinforcement creates the most reliable behaviors.

- Negative punishment is the best way to punish your dog.

- Make sure all of your dog's associations are pleasant ones.

Chapter

The Premack Principle

In This Chapter

🏠 What do you want your dog to do?

🏠 What your dog wants is pretty obvious

🏠 Teach your dog to *love* to behave

🏠 Consistency, consistency, consistency

The *Premack Principle* was developed by David Premack. It puts forth "The observation that high-probability behavior reinforces low-probability behavior." Essentially it means: "Eat your vegetables and you can have dessert." To make this a bit easier to understand in terms of dog training, high-probability behaviors are what the *dog* wants; low-probability behaviors are what *you* want. In this chapter, you'll learn how to use this principle to get the behaviors you want from your dog.

Eat Your Vegetables First: What You Want

So, what do you want from your dog? Think about this—really think. It's not easy, is it? Write it down if you have to. Come up with some concrete things you want from your dog. If you don't do this, you won't, well, know what you want from your dog! And if *you* don't know what you want, how the heck is *he* supposed to know? I know dogs are very smart and may seem to be "almost human," but as of yet, I don't believe dogs (or spouses or children) can really read your mind.

Do you want your dog to sit quietly at the door when the leash is being put on? How about calm behaviors when walking down the street? Perhaps bringing the ball and dropping it at your feet, rather than 20 feet away? Wouldn't you like to be able to peacefully sit and watch TV or prepare his food dish and put it on the floor without being mauled? Maybe you'd like him to stop straining at the leash to get to his doggie pal so that he can play. You *can* get all of these things and more, by finding out what your dog wants—what floats his boat.

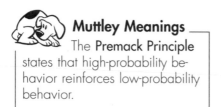

Muttley Meanings
The **Premack Principle** states that high-probability behavior reinforces low-probability behavior.

After you've thought it over, write down your goals—what you want from your dog. Now that you've written down what you want from your dog, it's time to figure out and write down what *he* wants.

Hot Fudge Sundae: What Does Your Dog Want?

How will you know what your dog wants? Watch him carefully and write down what he enjoys most. Don't think you'll remember it all without writing it down, because you won't. Humor me and write it down anyway. It'll come in handy later.

Canine Caveats
Be sure to pick only those things that you would want to use as reinforcers later. Sock stealing, paper eating, garbage raiding, poop eating, furniture rearranging or chewing, and general behaviors you don't want don't count and shouldn't be on this list.

Your dog might like to sniff; roll in smelly things; sniff; chase toys; play tug; play with other dogs; sniff; go swimming; go for a car ride; go for a walk, jog, or run; play in an open field; sniff; chase ducks, deer, or geese; herd sheep; find small rodents; be petted or massaged; sniff; do agility; cuddle with you; sniff; get belly rubs; retrieve objects; eat food; pee on bushes (hopefully yours and not the neighbor's); get attention from you; be groomed (my dogs like to be groomed); and last but not least, sniff.

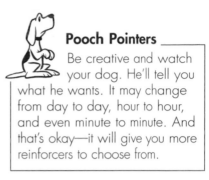

Pooch Pointers

Be creative and watch your dog. He'll tell you what he wants. It may change from day to day, hour to hour, and even minute to minute. And that's okay—it will give you more reinforcers to choose from.

At this time you should have two lists—one with what you want and one with what your dog wants. Now, let's put them together.

Making Everyone's Dreams Come True

The Premack Principle is often called "life rewards." Looking at your list of what the dog wants, you may start to get an inkling of how this is going to work. Make what your dog wants contingent upon doing what you want and you will be amazed and astounded at how quickly your dog performs behaviors!

Attention = Sheep Herding

Beau, one of my Border Collies, wanted to herd sheep. However, he thought I was irrelevant and was along only as a taxi driver. When herding sheep, it's important that the dog understand that he and his person are a team. He can't herd sheep without someone telling him what direction to go, and his person can't herd sheep without the dog doing his job.

Beau would drag me to the sheep pen. It was obvious by his inattentiveness to me that I didn't exist in his eyes. If I let him herd sheep anyway, he would ignore me and wouldn't take direction from me.

To teach him that focus on me made it possible to even enter the sheep pen, I insisted that he give me attention, heeling all the way from the car to the sheep pen. No attention meant no sheep. I would tie him to a post and leave. If he made movements toward me, I would come back to him. If his eye contact then wavered, I would leave again. There was no punishment, no anger, no letting him herd sheep, and no hard feelings. I just patiently waited for his attention.

It took him four "sheepless" sheep lessons to understand that he had to focus on me if he wanted to herd sheep. Once he learned this lesson, he was attentive outside the pen as well as inside.

Does Your Dog Own You?

You can make use of any of the things on your "what the dog wants" list to get what you want. Say you want to allow your dog to go swimming. You don't want him to drag you to the lake or pool. Make swimming dependent upon walking to the lake on a loose leash. No loose-leash walking, no swimming. If he doesn't walk nicely on the leash, just put him back in the car, wait for five to ten minutes, and try again. If, after three to four tries he still hasn't noticed that you're alive, take him back home.

Say you take your dog out to train or play, but he drags you from the car to the building or field. Enthusiasm is great, and that tells me you're doing a great job so far. However, you don't have to put up with inappropriate behaviors. Do the same thing as in the previous situation: no loose-leash walking, no fun stuff.

Do Become a Master Manipulator

Your dog wants you to throw the ball for him, but he drops it about 20 feet away. You want him to drop it at your feet, so don't go over to it, pick it up, and throw it. Wait for him to pick it up again and then back up. He should bring it closer this time. If he brings it a foot or two closer, then you can throw the ball. The next time, you may want him to drop the ball three feet closer. Wait for it to happen and then throw the ball for him. Continue so that he ends up dropping the ball at your feet. If he goes back to dropping it 20 feet away, then again, don't throw the ball.

Your dog wants to go out, but you don't want him to jump up and down like an idiot when you try to put on his collar and leash. Ignore his jumping and patiently wait. Once he's sitting calmly, put the leash on. If at any time, he starts jumping again, stand still and wait. If it takes 15 minutes, then so be it. He will very quickly learn that if he sits quietly, he'll get to go for a walk faster.

Canine Caveats

If you "give in" to your dog for any of these things, you're reinforcing the wrong behaviors. "Oh, but I drove all this way so he could swim." Too bad, bucko. If you're serious about wanting certain behaviors, then don't give in to the unacceptable behaviors you don't want.

Doggie Data

Sue's Australian Cattle Dog, Barney, wanted "sniffing" as his full-time job, so she put him on a "pay attention to me or you don't get to sniff" program.

Sue insisted on eye contact from Barney from the instant he left the car—she gave him 30 seconds to respond. If he ignored her, back into the car he went. Once he made eye contact within 30 seconds, she lowered the time and repeated this until Barney was responding within three seconds.

Sue would ask for some heeling, a sit, or a down. Then as a reward, she allowed Barney to sniff for a minute. If he didn't respond, he was put back into the car. Pretty soon, Barney was quickly responding to all sorts of cues—and sniffing less!

The key for Premacking anything is to know what your dog wants and then ask for what *you* want—be it calm behavior, eye contact, sits, downs, stays, or whatever it is you want from him at the time.

Pass the Lima Beans Please: Added Benefits

Let's say you have a dog that doesn't like to be touched. You can make touching a prerequisite to going outside. No touchy, no outside. Or no touchy, no ballie.

You don't have to start out with a full body rub. In fact, you shouldn't. Start with one light touch and then give the dog what he wants. Each day, you can add slightly more petting until you're eventually giving the dog a bear hug and he's actually liking the handling.

The neat thing about Premacking is that the dog will very often learn to enjoy whatever behavior it is that you want. This is what "reinforcing low-probability behavior" means. The less likely of the two behaviors actually takes on more meaning to the dog. Now you have yet another way to reinforce your dog!

Pooch Pointers

My Sheltie Cody actually likes toenail clipping because I Premacked it with stuff he wanted.

Doggie Data

Todd's dog Jesse hated to be handled in any way, but loved tennis balls. By lightly touching each and every body part before throwing the ball, over the course of a few months, Todd was able to groom and pet Jesse. In fact, Jesse learned to love petting so much that not only was Todd able to handle his dog, but their entire relationship changed for the better.

A dolphin at SeaWorld was in serious need of fresh water. The only way to accommodate this need was through a stomach tube, but the dolphin had to be trained to accept this within five days, otherwise it was going to die.

The trainers not only taught the dolphin to accept the stomach tube, they did their job so well that the dolphin ended up *liking* the stomach tube—so much so that he *wanted* it as a reward! Now, how's *that* for the ultimate in Premack?! Did I get your creative juices flowing? What will you train your dog to *love*?

Green Means Stop, Red Means Go: Give Consistent Cues

Premack can backfire *only* if you're inconsistent. If sometimes you give in and sometimes you hold your ground, then guess what? Premack won't work for you. And your dog will still be pulling you on the leash, sniffing nonstop, or doing all the things that drive you insane. In fact, no dog training will work for you if you're inconsistent. Inconsistency is extremely frustrating for your dog, just as it is for humans.

How would you feel if today on the news it was announced that tomorrow, all green lights meant stop and all red lights meant go? We've been programmed to know the opposite, so, even though we speak English, and understood the change in rules, we'd probably make many mistakes tomorrow. Accidents would happen and we'd get very angry.

Think how your dog feels. He doesn't speak English. Really. You only think he does. So, if today, "Come On" means come and tomorrow, "Let's Go" means come, and the next day "Come" means loose-leash walking, and the day after that "Comecomecomecome" means come … well, you can see how frustrating that can be to your dog and why your dog ignores you a lot of the time.

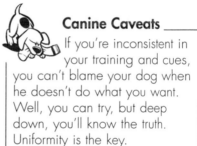

Canine Caveats

If you're inconsistent in your training and cues, you can't blame your dog when he doesn't do what you want. Well, you can try, but deep down, you'll know the truth. Uniformity is the key.

The Least You Need to Know

- If you know what behavior *you* want from your dog, you can get that behavior by rewarding him with something you know *he* wants.

- Before the dog gets what he wants, he must do what you want.

- Using Premacking, the dog will very often learn to enjoy the behavior that you want him to do.

- Consistency is the secret to successful Premacking.

Chapter 7

Are You Listening to What Your Dog Is Telling You?

In This Chapter

- 🏠 The canine peacekeeping system
- 🏠 Stop stressing out your dog!
- 🏠 Dog talk and how to recognize it
- 🏠 Use this knowledge to your benefit

Dogs are pack animals and it's important for animals that live in a pack (wolves, dogs, humans) to have ritualized methods for avoiding aggression and conflict. Every species on this planet owns its own set of rules and regulations. Dogs give out 47 signals that we humans can perceive. There are 10 signals that we give to dogs that the dogs perceive as aggressive or threatening.

This chapter shows you the signals your dog is trying to give you, and also tells you what signals you might be sending back without realizing it. Then you'll learn some ways to communicate using the dog's own language.

Why Dogs Give Off Precursor Signals

We all possess certain signs or *precursors* that signify "I won't hurt you, I am a nice wolf/dog/person." We must learn to inhibit our aggression—otherwise the pack will not survive. If there were no stopgaps, we'd all just kill each other and die out as a species.

In this country, direct eye contact and hands reaching out to shake hands are seen as proper greeting behavior. If someone refused to look at you or shake your hand, you'd feel uncomfortable or possibly suspicious. In other countries, direct eye contact and shaking hands might be perceived as a threat or the height of bad manners.

 Muttley Meanings

A **precursor** is a sign that something is going to happen. This can be a signal that the dog is getting nervous or a sign that something good is going to happen, such as the rattle of a plastic bag, signifying that a dog treat is coming.

 Doggie Data

While dogs have some threatening signs—growling, barking, lunging, teeth bared—they have more signals to avoid conflict.

Just as people from different cultures don't always understand each other's signals, people have trouble interpreting the signals that dogs give out. Human reactions to these signals, such as always blaming the owner, always blaming the dog, putting the dog down, keeping the dog locked up, or keeping the kids locked up (my personal favorite) all get in the way of understanding that dogs have a very specific culture that does not equate with our human culture.

How can we avert serious, antagonistic events involving our dogs?

> **Canine Caveats**
>
> We must put dogs and their doggie behaviors into perspective.
>
> 🐾 Dogs behave like dogs because they're not fuzzy kids with four legs.
>
> 🐾 Most humans don't understand dog behavior, because we're not naked dogs with only two legs.
>
> 🐾 Dogs misinterpret our behavior and we misinterpret their behavior.

Understanding Your Dog's Precursor Signs

Because dogs are dogs, they don't have morals or ethics, feel guilt or shame. Why? Because dogs are dogs! These are human emotions and dogs are a different species. However, dogs do have a very strict system of manners with fitting responses.

We humans are for the most part clueless regarding these behavioral responses because we're not dogs. An inability to communicate effectively with dogs is the overwhelming cause for almost every canine "behavior" problem. It's really a human problem, not a dog problem.

In doggie land, communication is accomplished through a series of complex sounds, facial and body movements, and scent. The combination changes all of the time and the meanings are different each time. If the first sequence of signs is ignored, they will increase in severity and additional behaviors will appear.

 Doggie Data

Imagine that you brought your child, at eight weeks of age, into the wild and dumped him or her in the woods for a wolf pack to raise. Sounds pretty silly, doesn't it? Well, we're doing the same thing when we bring a puppy into our households. The food is different, the language is different, and the rules are different. We expect miracles from our dogs.

> **Doggie Data** ___
> Marshall brought his seven-year-old Boxer, Brandy, to see me. Brandy had been biting Marshall's one-year-old son in the face. Marshall loved his dog and was determined to fix this problem. By teaching Marshall the dog's signals, he was able to move his son away from the dog before the signals escalated. Within three weeks, the dog had completely stopped bothering the little boy.

For instance, a child or adult is doing something that the dog regards as threatening. The dog may signal, nonverbally at first, that he's not happy with your behavior. The adult or child doesn't notice and continues to pressure the dog.

The dog may use additional nonverbal signals and is ignored again. And again. The dog's signals may now include some verbal noises, such as a low growl. If the warnings are continually ignored, and the dog has been unable to make his point politely (within his own frame of reference), the dog's signals will escalate into lifting his lip, snarling, showing teeth, and snapping or biting.

> **Doggie Data** ___
> Lisa was volunteering in a shelter for homeless dogs. Shelters are very stressful places and she wanted to help reduce their stress. After learning to recognize these signals, she utilized them during her visits. Within a few days, the dogs in the kennels were barking less, calming down faster, and were able to focus better during the retraining process.

These types of behaviors that seemingly came "out of nowhere," didn't come out of nowhere—you just weren't paying attention.

Is Your Dog Stressed?

As we know, life in general is stressful. Some stress is good and some can be devastating—both mentally and physically. Teaching your dog to accept a certain amount of anxiety is vital in creating a happy and healthy dog that will bounce back quickly from everyday stressful events. The more common causes of stress are listed below. Some of them we can forestall and prevent; some we can't.

Stressed-Out Puppies

Here are some possible causes of stress for puppies:

- Stressed mother

- Born into a puppy mill—including being taken away from mom and siblings too soon, the truck ride, and the pet shop

- Environment change (even when you get the dog from a reputable breeder)

- Isolation or lack of proper food, water, or social contact (dogs are pack animals)

- Tail docking, ear cropping, dewclaw removal

- Travel

- Socializing the dog improperly or not at all

Stress for Adult Dogs

Here are some causes of stress for adult dogs:

- Moving, being given up for adoption, dumped, abandoned

- Suddenly taking the dog to new places without training him to accept distractions with positive results in a variety of situations

- Competitive dog sports, such as agility (see Chapter 19)

- Not having been socialized as a puppy

- Sickness

- Too little or too much exercise

- Punishment

- Grooming

- Dissension in pack (human or canine)

🏠 Being "corrected" (a politically correct word for punishment) every time they give the owner precursor signs that they are nervous ("please don't be angry with me"), which makes them confused and frustrated

🏠 Inconsistency in training.

🏠 Bitches coming into heat—stressful for both the bitch and any males that are around

A Brand New Language: What the 47 Dog Signals Are

The following are 47 perceptible precursor signals that dogs give off:

🏠 Head turning away

🏠 Howling

(Photo by P. Dennison)

Head turn, lip licking, and paw raised in avoidance.

🏠 Eyes turning away

🏠 Growling

- Yawning
- Spinning/circling
- Panting, heavy breathing
- Stopped or frozen (in an awkward position)
- Drooling
- Sniffing

(Photo by P. Dennison)

Sniffing when play becomes too rough.

- Lip licking
- Short attention span
- Raising a paw (as if to "Shake")

- Biting the leash
- Whining
- Poop eating
- Barking
- Grass eating
- Water drinking
- Marking
- Pooping
- Aggression
- Avoidance

(Photo by P. Dennison)

Head down and moving away in avoidance.

(Photo by P. Dennison)

Two dogs studiously avoiding each other.

- Hyper behavior

- Slow, reluctant behaviors

- Complete body turns away from you

- Play bows

- *Arcing* (or curving)

Muttley Meanings _____

When dogs approach each other and wish to avoid fights, they **arc** around each other rather than approach head on. They will arc in a big circle, at times even curving their bodies. This can calm the other dog and avoid a potential conflict.

(Photo by P. Dennison)

Two dogs meet and one dog arcs (curves) her body.

🏠 Sitting

🏠 Laying down

(Photo by P. Dennison)

Enticing another dog to play by offering a submissive down.

(Photo by P. Dennison)

Rolling over in submission: "Don't eat me!".

- 🐾 Frantically wagging tail

- 🐾 Shaking (as if they were shaking off water)

- 🐾 *Hackles* raised

- 🐾 *Splitting*

 Muttley Meanings

When one dog runs between two other dogs that are playing rough, he's **splitting.** He splits from the rear for obvious reasons (there are no teeth in the rear). Dogs often split up humans, too. This isn't jealousy; it's the dog's perception that the closeness is dangerous. **Hackles** are the hair along the spine or neck. The dog 's hackles raise up when he is nervous.

(Photo by P. Dennison)

Splitting up too rough play.

- Blinking the eyes

- Body shaking (as if they are cold)

- Sneezing

- Scratching

- Sweaty paws

- Raised pulse rate

- Raised temperature (ears can get hot)

- "Stress" shedding and dandruff

- Chewing

- Digging

- Diarrhea

- Loss of appetite (won't take treats)

(Photo by P. Dennison)

The Border Collie is lifting his lip. The Schnauzer is very stiff.

🏠 Head lowered

🏠 Showing teeth

Ambiguous Signals

Many of the precursor signals just listed are natural, normal behaviors, so you have to look at the context in which the dog is doing those things. If the dog has just finished playing or if it's a hot day, drinking would be a normal behavior. If, however, you've asked your dog to do something that he's stressed about, water drinking would be a sign that he's nervous.

Grass eating is usually a sign of one of three things:

🏠 The dog has an upset tummy and he needs to throw up (and will most likely do so on your bed).

🏠 The dog is missing some nutrients from his diet.

🏠 The dog is stressed.

Dogs will often "graze" when meeting someone new (be it a person or another dog).

A play bow can be an invitation to play, or it can be a sign of nervousness. I always look at the other dog to see what the play bow really means. If the other dog then plays, the bow was intended to entice. If the other dog goes off sniffing or doing other behaviors, the bow was presented as an "I am nervous" signal.

(Photo by P. Dennison)

One dog enticing another dog to play utilizing a play bow.

Yawning and lip licking can also have two meanings. They can be natural—the dog is tired and yawns, or he's drawing in scent by licking. Or they can be signs of stress.

Personal Stress Signals

In addition, there are also what I call "personal" precursor signals. These are different for every dog:

🏠 The set of his ears and tail

🏠 Any creases on his face

- The shape of his nose and muzzle, which often changes when a dog feels stressed
- The look and shape of his eyes and pupils
- Foaming at the mouth (different than drooling)
- Tightness of his mouth when taking food
- Suppleness or tightness of his body and face
- Puffing out of cheeks with short but explosive breaths

(Photo by P. Dennison)

Lip licking.

Every dog is a little different. Some dogs have cropped ears or tails and so some of these signals don't apply. Some dogs show their nervousness by enlargement of their pupils, but in some dogs it's the complete opposite—their pupils get very tiny.

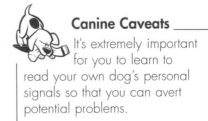

Canine Caveats

It's extremely important for you to learn to read your own dog's personal signals so that you can avert potential problems.

How Rude! Twelve Human Signals

Most of these signals we humans don't even think about when approaching dogs—any dog, be it our own or a strange dog. Others are tenets of negative training philosophies. I hope you will think about them now, because you might be stressing your dog out continually, which is an accident waiting to happen.

Here are the stressful signals you might be giving your dog:

- Leaning over the dog
- Forcing your face in the dog's face
- Petting the dog on the withers (shoulder blade) area
- Petting the dog around the face and especially on the top of the head
- Walking straight into the dog
- Eye contact (with a strange dog)
- Hands reaching down to the dog

Here are five of the threatening postures that relate to punishment-based training methods. You won't do these anymore, will you?

- "Alpha" rolls
- Scruff shakes
- Hitting
- Yelling
- Forcing the dog into position (such as a "Sit" or "Down")

Can you teach your dogs to accept the first 7 human signals without becoming fearful or aggressive? Of course you can, and you must. It is imperative to teach your dog to accept all types of obnoxious human behavior. If you don't, you're headed for some big problems.

(Photo by P. Dennison)

Person leaning over a dog in an inappropriate way.

Canine Caveats

Some people may tell you that you have to be "dominant over your dog," "show 'em who's boss," or that you should "be the alpha." They're assuming that you need to punish your dog to be in control. This will only get you into trouble by creating other far-reaching problems—aggression, avoidance, or shy behaviors.

Humans can't replicate a true canine alpha. By incorrectly viewing aggressive behaviors as the proper way to rule our dogs, we can't expect our dogs to be happy and willing participants in our relationship. Be your dogs' benevolent leader, not a malevolent dictator. Rule by kindness and consistency. Be clear about what you want and you'll never need to dominate your dog into submission.

What Can I Do to Reduce My Dog's Stress?

Except for the more disgusting things such as marking, poop eating, grass eating, and the like, we humans can communicate directly to our dogs using the same language they use. You can very effectively use the following in most cases:

- Avert your eyes
- Avert your face
- Turn your back on the dog
- Walk slowly away
- Freeze in position
- Yawn
- Lick your lips
- Sit
- Lie down
- Kneel on the ground and pluck grass
- Turn sideways
- Blink
- Split
- Arc or curve
- Walk parallel to the dog

Instead of forcing ourselves on dogs, we can use these signs to entice them to come to us. A typical greeting can be the following:

- Glance in the dog's direction and quickly avert your eyes, or even blink a few times.
- While looking away, lick your lips and/or yawn.

- Glance back again, then turn your head and body away from the dog.

- Move away slowly for a few steps.

- Squat or kneel down, turning your body sideways to the dog.

- Keep your hands to yourself. Let your arms drop naturally by your side and wait for the dog to approach.

If at any time the dog sniffs the ground, avoids you, yawns, or licks his lips, you may answer him back with some of your own signals. Be sure to discontinue the approach and just move away slowly. Never pressure a dog to say "hello." That's just setting the dog up to be more nervous or fearful.

By learning these signals, becoming fluent in "dog," and practicing them yourselves, you can effectively learn to communicate with your dog and avert potential disasters.

The Least You Need to Know

- Dogs give off signals to keep the peace.

- We unknowingly do things that stress our dogs, and they try to tell us not to.

- Be aware of your dog's signals to avoid potential problems.

- Humans can use dog signals to communicate with dogs and avoid disaster.

How Will Knowing My Dog's Signals Help Me Train Him?

In This Chapter

- 🏠 Is your dog stressed?
- 🏠 Managing stressful situations
- 🏠 Set your dog up to succeed
- 🏠 By watching your dog, you can avoid potential problems

By always keeping an eye on your dog and heeding the multitude of signals he's giving you about his emotional state, you can avoid potential problems. If you ignore a dog's fear signals and pressure him, he not only will learn to fear that object (and react by either aggressing or running away), but will also lose his language because it's being ignored—it doesn't "work" anymore.

Sense and Sensibility: Watch for the Signs of Stress

If your dog is stressed and you don't know it, you might instead believe you have a stupid or stubborn dog because of his behavior. He may be nervous about a new location or new people, but you believe he's being "bad" when he ignores you. So, you end up jerking him around and in effect punishing him for being afraid.

When a dog loses his ability to tell you that he's anxious, this is a very dangerous thing. Without the means to give off the early warning signs (also called *precursors*) of nervousness, a dog is more likely to go directly to the more serious aspects of warning—growling and biting.

Learn to read your dog for signs of stress. If a child or stranger is approaching and your dog exhibits early signs of stress (lip licking, head turning, backing away, etc.), don't allow the person to approach any closer. Allowing a person to continue to approach will either put the dog into a more defensive posture or cause him to be more afraid and try to run away.

Growling

A growl is an important mode of communication from the dog to you. It's not aggression—it's a warning. When the police say, "Stop or I'll shoot," this doesn't mean that they will shoot regardless of what you do or don't do; it's a warning.

 Doggie Data

When I was a groomer, if a dog growled at me I would praise him and give him treats. Why? Because he warned me that if I continued, I was going to get bloody. As a result, I was never bitten.

If you punish a dog for growling, you deny yourself a warning that your dog is feeling threatened. If you're smart, you'll thank your dog for growling because he's just letting you know that he's very uncomfortable, and if you don't stop what you're doing, he may bite you. A growling dog doesn't want to bite you—that's why he's growling as a warning.

Don't Punish the Warning Signs!

Dogs learn by association. If you punish a dog for growling, the dog learns to associate the bad feeling the punishment gave him with that other object—be it another dog, person, or child. The dog already felt some anxiety or fear about that object to start off with, and now your punishment made him even more fearful.

If you haven't done anything to train an alternative behavior or *desensitize* the dog to that object, the next time he comes in contact with that object, those bad feelings will occur again—perhaps stronger this time. The dog will be even more anxiety ridden in the presence of that stimuli and will feel an even greater need to be defensive. But now he can't even tell you because you punished him for giving his warning signs. And because he was punished for growling, he may go directly to biting without a warning.

Muttley Meanings

Desensitization or **systematic desensitization**—a form of counterconditioning, a procedure in which a phobic subject (human or animal) is subjected to low levels of the frightening stimulus while relaxed. The level of frightening stimulus is gradually increased, but never at a rate to cause distress. Eventually, the fear dissipates.

Counterconditioning—The use of associative learning to reverse the unwanted effects of prior conditioning.

If the dog is growling at you, *please*, please, pretty please don't take it personally. Your dog is just telling you that he doesn't like whatever it is you're doing. There may be an underlying cause—physical or mental—of the growling. Perhaps you hurt him inadvertently or he has a boo-boo that you didn't see.

Muttley Meanings
Provoking stimuli are things your dog is afraid of. These can include people, dogs, cows, horses, fence posts, drainpipes, petting in inappropriate ways, the vacuum cleaner—basically anything that makes the dog nervous.

Make sure there's no hidden reason and then use the growl as a wake-up call to then train the dog to accept whatever it is that made him unhappy. If you see these signs, you must desensitize and *countercondition* your dog to any *provoking stimuli*.

Cease and Desist: Stopping Bad Behaviors in Stressful Situations

You can (and should) stop "bad" behaviors before they start or escalate. It's extremely important to learn to detect the subtle signals of stress and intervene on your dog's behalf. Waiting to do something until your dog is in full defense mode is counterproductive. Dogs in defense are aroused, their heart rate is high, their *adrenaline* and *glucocorticoid* levels are high, and it takes two to six days for these stress hormones to come down to normal levels. Until then, the dog is incapable of learning.

Muttley Meanings
Adrenaline and **glucocorticoids** are hormones produced in mammals during stress to help the body prepare for a fight-or-flight response.

Any added stressor that the dog comes into contact with before the hormone levels go back to normal will set the dog's stress clock even higher and the dog may react even more vehemently.

Strange People Approaching Your Dog

If a stranger approaches you and your dog and your dog gets nervous, tell the other person to stop his or her approach, or simply walk away from the person. The general public doesn't own your dog and there's no law that I know of that insists that the general public be allowed to pet your dog.

Pooch Pointers

Some people might insist on approaching your nervous dog, perhaps saying "Oh, it's okay, I have dogs at home," or some other such nonsense. It's up to you, the owner, to keep your dog safe from people like this. You wouldn't allow a stranger to approach and touch your child, would you? Of course not. So don't allow strangers to approach, especially when your dog has already shown that he's nervous.

There is some weird old wives' tale that says you must reach out a hand to let the dog sniff you and after that, it is okay for you to pet him on the head. Like most old wive's tales, this is wrong! As we learned, the dog sees this as threatening. The proper thing to do is to crouch down to the dog's level and let him sniff you at his own pace.

(Photo by P. Dennison)

Proper greeting etiquette from the human.

Dog-to-Dog Confrontations

Let dogs give their signals to each other, rather than forcing "obedience." If your dog is nervous about another dog, don't force him to walk close to the other dog—arc around at a distance so both dogs feel comfortable.

Not every dog has to be friends with every other dog. My preference is that my dogs be *calm* around all other dogs, rather than expect playmates in all the dogs we meet. After all, we don't like every person we meet, either.

Leashes

You can inadvertently teach your dog to be aggressive by the way you use your leash. You should use the leash as a safety net, not as a tool. Your relationship is what should control the dog. Leashes can break or be yanked out of your hand, and collars break, too. If you use the leash as a tool, you really don't have a relationship with your dog.

Muttley Meanings

Redirect or redirected aggression means to take an emotion a dog or human can't express in a situation and direct it toward another object, human, or dog. For example, your boss yells at you and you can't yell back because you need your job. So, to alleviate the stress you're feeling, you yell at co-workers, the drivers on the way home, and anyone who gets in your way.

If you continually yank on your dog, you're stressing him and he can't concentrate on anything other than "What is this pressure on my neck? Stop yanking me!" He then may *redirect* onto the next object he sees.

A dog on a leash, just by virtue of being confined, is in a defensive mode—he can't escape danger and he knows it. That's why so many dogs are aggressive when they're on a leash.

If you yank your dog away from another dog, the state of arousal becomes higher and higher until what perhaps started as a simple,

"Hi, who are you, what's your name?" can quickly become, "Come any closer and I'll rip your throat out!" If your dog doesn't yet walk on a loose leash around other dogs, avoid the company of other dogs until you've trained more. You can certainly do some off-leash work if the other dogs are friendly and the area is safe. See Chapter 13 for a full discussion of training your dog on the leash.

Doggie Data

When I was a groomer, a lovely, well-adjusted, happy Springer Spaniel, who came in often, all of a sudden one day started growling at me, and his eyes were very scary. When his owners came to pick him up, I explained what had happened and asked about any changes in the household, diet, or health. They'd also noticed a slight change in the dog's behavior, and upon further examination, learned that the new babysitter was abusing both the dog and their grandson.

The moral? Don't ever punish your dog for growling—listen to what he's saying. I knew the aggressive display was out of character. Because I didn't let it go, the dog and child were saved from a bad situation.

The best way to introduce dogs to each other is in a safe, enclosed area with leashes off and only two dogs at a time. A great deal of tension travels down the leash from you right to the dog. If you're nervous, the dog will be nervous and stressed about the other dog, too.

Slow Down, You Move Too Fast: Better Ways of Coping with Stress

Fearful behaviors are self-reinforcing because those behaviors keep the scary thing away. If the beginning stages of fear don't keep the scary thing away, the level of fear will increase into aggression or avoidance until the behavior (from the dog's point of view) is successful in protecting him.

Canine Caveats

Comforting the fearful dog backfires because you're actually not comforting the dog—you're reinforcing the fearful behavior. On the other hand, punishing the fearful dog creates a more fearful dog who may then escalate into aggression. A better idea is to ignore the behavior completely. Wait for the dog to become calm and then reinforce the calm behaviors.

Alternative Behaviors

The best thing you can do is to teach your dog alternative behaviors to being nervous. Teach him basic obedience, such as attention, eye contact, loose-leash walking, interactive play with you, name recognition, coming when you call, or even just standard pet tricks to name a few. Anything that keeps the dog from obsessing toward the feared object counts.

Get Out of the Bad Situation

In the beginning, if the dog is already in a frenzy, get him out of the situation. If you can catch him before he goes berserk, you can learn to calm him down without getting frustrated and without accidentally reinforcing the dog. Accidental reinforcement of "bad" behaviors is probably the most common cause of behavioral problems in dogs. That's why it's so important to be able to read your dog and set him up to be right.

Human Body Postures That Calm

Once you become fluent in "dog," you'll be able to stop the behavior almost before it starts. Here are some ways to calm a dog using your body and his language:

🏠 Put the dog in an area where there are no prey objects or other stress-inducing stimuli in the dog's line of sight or hearing.

🏠 Stand upright, facing the same direction as the dog. You can also turn your back on the dog or just twist your body away.

🏠 Avoid eye contact, unless the dog is seeking your eye contact—then acknowledge his glance calmly, momentarily. If you've taught him that calm eye contact gets him what he wants, so much the better. You can then blink your eyes, avert your gaze, or turn your head away.

Doggie Data

Cynthia was teaching a group class when all of a sudden one of the dogs began to bark. The other dogs in the class decided that was a great idea and also started barking. Cynthia asked the owners (over the din) to start yawning and licking their lips. Within 60 seconds, all of the dogs were quiet and ready to refocus on the lesson.

(Photo by P. Dennison)

A person turning her body to avoid the dog.

(Photo by P. Dennison)

A person turning her head to avoid looking at the dog.

Canine Caveats

When petting your dog, make sure you're not reinforcing the "bad" behavior. The better bet is to pet him *before* he gets nervous, or *after* he calms down, reinforcing the calm behavior.

🏠 Speak in a soft and calm voice, or be silent—silence is best. You can also yawn or lick your lips.

🏠 Move calmly and slowly, or freeze in position.

🏠 Pet the dog, but be sure to pet along the back and sides in long, soothing strokes with a very light touch.

United We Stand: Set the Dog Up for Success

If your dog shows signs of fear or nervousness (review the signs in Chapter 7), don't set him up to be fearful. Limit his access to the feared objects and slowly, methodically go in closer while reinforcing for calm behaviors.

Eeek! A Plastic Reindeer!

If your dog is nervous about inanimate objects—swing sets, rowboats, plastic reindeer, and the like—don't laugh; just stand still while he makes a fool of himself. You can place treats all around the object and let the dog move closer at his own pace.

If your dog is nervous about having company over, put him in a separate room until you can take the time to train him to accept company. If your dog jumps on people coming to the door, put him on leash while you open the door and reinforce him for sitting. If your dog has problems with kids and bikes going past the picture window, close the curtains.

Please Teach Me to Like Head Petting!

If your dog doesn't like petting on the head (ninety-nine percent of all dogs don't like it), then, until you train him to like it, don't pet him on the head. Think your dog does? Try this test: Call him over to you and pet him on the head. If he avoids your touch, ducks his head, moves away completely, or moves his head toward your hand (as if to bite—even without a show of teeth), well, guess what? Your dog is part of the 99th percentile and is completely normal.

Doggie Data

Louise came in with her dog Teddy, with her arms bloody and scratched. Teddy didn't like petting at all and would tell her so in a not-nice way. After one week of working with Teddy, he allowed Louise to pet him. We taught him to enjoy petting by pairing a light touch with treats (the Premack principle). After the second week, Teddy was actively enjoying having Louise pet him. (See more about the Premack principle in Chapter 6.)

Can we teach our dogs to accept inappropriate behaviors from strangers, and inappropriate handling by veterinarians? Of course we can, and we *must!* It's important to remember, though, that dogs don't naturally like certain behaviors and we should view them as we would view any behavior that isn't natural for a dog—*train it!* Specific guidelines for teaching your dog to accept handling are addressed in Chapter 11.

(Photo by P. Dennison)

A dog trained to accept threatening body postures from humans.

Until you can take the time to train your dog to accept the human world in all its complexities, manage the situations as best you can so that your dog doesn't practice nervous or fearful behaviors. After all, practice makes perfect, whether the behavior is "good" or "bad."

Get Your Dog's Attention

When you want to attract your dog away from something else more interesting, think like prey. Dogs are attracted to movement because they're predators! Here's what to do:

🏠 Your body posture should be low to the ground and approach sideways. Be careful not to loom over the dog because this is perceived as aggressive. You can lean backwards, wave your arms, wiggle your fingers, or run away.

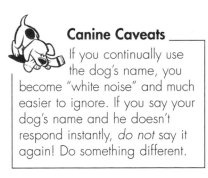

Canine Caveats

If you continually use the dog's name, you become "white noise" and much easier to ignore. If you say your dog's name and he doesn't respond instantly, *do not* say it again! Do something different.

🏠 Avoid direct eye contact or give a sideways glance.

🏠 Use a high-pitched, excited, squeaky voice or even a whistle. Loud, deep voices do the opposite—they repel dogs.

🏠 Move side to side or away from the dog—the faster the better. Feint right and left—act really exciting!

🏠 Play with whatever toys your dog really likes.

🏠 You can do some mild roughhousing with the dog, to energize but not overstimulate him.

Pooch Pointers

What else can you do to ensure that your dog grows up with a healthy attitude in this complex world we live in? You can educate yourself, your family, and your friends about canine behavior and body language. You can get the pups out and about, as much as possible, from the time they're eight weeks old, always moving at their pace and their comfort level. You can teach your puppies manners and acceptance of the human species they now live with. You can always observe, watch over, and listen to your dog—in his language.

The Least You Need to Know

🏠 Watch your dog at all times for signs of stress or fear—and *do not* punish these signs.

🏠 Learn to manage your dog's stressful situations, such as meeting other dogs and people and being on a leash.

🏠 Use your leash as a safety net, not to drag your dog around.

🏠 Learn and watch for your dog's precursors to nervousness to avoid problems.

Chapter 9

Slots, Soda, and Hawaii: Reinforcements

In This Chapter

- 🏠 You can be boring or you can be impulsive
- 🏠 Variety is the spice of life
- 🏠 Surprise! Here's a ticket to Bermuda!
- 🏠 Plan to be the best trainer you can be

Behaviorist B.F. Skinner discovered three reinforcement schedules for animal training. Two of them will create a bored, lazy, and noncompliant dog. Use only those two and you may hear your dog say, "Yeah, sure, when I feel like it." But, if you use the variable schedule of reinforcement, you'll be sure to get, "Sure! When? Yesterday? No problemo!" Add in surprise elements and there is no limit to what you and your dog can accomplish.

It's a Shell Game: Different Reinforcement Schedules

B.F. Skinner was the first to discover how variable reinforcement schedules can actually increase or decrease specific behaviors. Skinner came upon this marvel of observable fact when he was running out of rat pellets during experiments and the rats still performed behaviors, at a stable rate, for less food. Wahoo!

He called it "schedules of reinforcement," and it opened up a whole new area of study for him and others in behavioral psychology. The study of it spread to marine mammal trainers and then dog trainers (and sometimes even human trainers).

There are three different types of reinforcement schedules that can be used for training: continuous, fixed, and variable. Some are more effective than others in maintaining or advancing behaviors. Some actually kill behaviors.

Continuous Reinforcement

Continuous reinforcement was the original method Skinner practiced, meaning that for every correct behavior, a treat was delivered. This schedule is great for teaching new behaviors.

You can see continuous schedules of reinforcement in your daily life. When you first learned to use a vending machine, it was very reinforcing to put our money in and out popped a prize. This encouraged you to do it again when you wanted something to eat or drink.

Fixed Schedule of Reinforcement Slows Down Learning

There are two types of fixed schedules: fixed interval and fixed ratio. With a fixed-interval schedule, the food is fed at specific *times*, rather than for specific behaviors. If your dog does one sit in a 20-second period, he gets one treat. If he doesn't sit, he doesn't get a treat. But even if he sits 100 times in 20 seconds, he still gets one treat. One interesting thing that happens is that the dog will pace himself by slowing down the rate of his behavior right after the reinforcer, and speed up again when the time for it gets close.

You call your dog from the back yard to no avail. You call at 10 A.M., you call at noon, and you call at 3 P.M. No doggie. However, at 5 P.M., you call your dog and he comes flying. Why? Because you always feed him his dinner at 5 P.M. He knows that no reinforcement is coming at those other times, so he doesn't come.

> **Canine Caveats**
>
> Stick to a fixed-interval schedule and you'll get what's called scalloping. Say you're having the dog heel and you give him a treat every five seconds (because we humans are creatures of habit). The dog may, after taking the treat, go off and sniff and then run back after three or four seconds to get his next "fix."

> **Doggie Data**
>
> Kathy fed her dogs exactly at 5 P.M., and they would whine and bark a few minutes before that time. To try to stop this obnoxious behavior, she went on a random schedule of feeding, changing the time each day. Unfortunately for Kathy, the dogs started to whine and bark all day because they never knew when they'd be fed.
>
> This is a perfect example of how changing the time between reinforcers can increase the behaviors. I never said the behaviors would always be good ones! What actually happened is that Kathy was inadvertently reinforcing the whining and barking by continuing to feed the dogs in spite of the unwanted behavior, thus reinforcing the very thing she wanted to extinguish.

A different type of fixed schedule is the fixed-ratio schedule, which reinforces the dog after so many behaviors on a regular schedule. The dog sits 3, 6, or 20 times and always gets a cookie after the third, sixth, or twentieth time. The number of behaviors asked for remains the same between reinforcers in a fixed-ratio schedule.

Pooch Pointers

Because they're predictable, fixed-interval and fixed-ratio schedules can create boredom and dullness in your dog and an unwillingness to perform.

Fixed-interval and fixed-ratio schedules can kill behaviors in dogs as well as humans. Fixed ratios are predictable, and predictability is boring, tedious, dreary, and mind numbing.

Okay, so you get the point on how predictability kills behavior. What's the answer? Variable reinforcement, of course!

Eenie, Meenie, Minie, Mo: Variable Reinforcement

Skinner also looked at two different types of variable reinforcement schedules: variable ratio and variable interval. A variable ratio means you change the number of behaviors needed each time. First it takes 3 sits to get a treat, then 10, then 1, then 7, and so on.

Canine Caveats

Before you bet 10 dollars that your dog will do any behavior you ask for, you need to move from continuous reinforcement (treating for every correct performance of the behavior) to a variable schedule of reinforcement. After the first, let's say, 10 sits, stop reinforcing for each one. Otherwise, your dog will sit only if you have a treat in your hand. Contrary to what you might think, giving your dog a treat every time doesn't make for strong and reliable behaviors.

Variable interval means you keep changing the time period between reinforcements—first 20 seconds, then 5, then 35, then 10, and so on. As a result, dogs no longer pace themselves, because they no can no longer establish a rhythm between behavior and reward.

Both variable ratio and variable interval keep dogs on their toes. But most important, these schedules are very resistant to *behavior extinction*. It makes sense if you think about it. In the dog's mind, if he hasn't gotten a reinforcer for a while, well, it just might come if he does just one more sit!

Muttley Meanings
Behavior extinction
occurs when a behavior is not reinforced anymore and so the behavior stops.

When the Soda Machine Suddenly Becomes a Slot Machine

When you put money in a slot machine, you might not win very often, but you never know whether and when you'll win again. You also don't know how much you'll win—it could be 25 cents or $500. You just might win the very next time, and if you don't try one more time, you might possibly miss on the score of the century!

This is just the opposite of how a vending machine works. You put your money in and a soda comes out. So what happens if you put your money in and nothing comes out? There are a few options you might consider:

🏠 Walk away

🏠 Put in more money and try one more time

🏠 Find a sledgehammer and beat it to death

Now, look at this from your dog's point of view. If you get stuck on a continuous reinforcement schedule and all of a sudden you try to be more variable, your dog's possible reactions could include the following:

🏠 Walk away

🏠 Try to sit again, just to make sure the cookie machine isn't broken

🏠 Bark, whine, or bite in frustration because the cookie machine isn't paying out

Variety: The Spice of Your Dog's Life

Add reinforcement variety to variable reinforcement schedules (interval or ratio) and you're home free for life! Variable reinforcement with reinforcement variety is the strongest schedule for maintaining a behavior.

Variety is just that—variety of reinforcement type. The key is not to use the same old thing to reinforce the dog. Reinforcement variety not only makes strong behaviors; it also helps enrich the dog's life. Here are some examples of reinforcers you can use:

🏠 **Food:** chicken, cheese, hot dogs, liverwurst, tortellini, steak, chickpeas, kidney beans, liver brownies, kibble, burnt leftovers that no one wants, vegetables, fruit; the list is endless.

🏠 **Toys:** tennis balls, Frisbees, tug toys, kongs; anything your dog likes to play with (Exception: Don't use old shoes or socks as toys because the dog will get the idea that your new socks and shoes are also toys.)

🏠 **Activities:** swimming, car rides, walks in the woods, tag you're it, chasing you, jogging, hiking, grooming (some dogs *do* like being groomed), playing with other dogs

Canine Caveats

It is too easy to get stuck using food as your only reinforcement type. Using variable schedules and variable types of reinforcement makes you use creativity, imagination, and forethought.

🏠 **"Life rewards":** sniffing that pile of poop, rolling in smelly things, chasing squirrels (in a safe area, please!), peeing on bushes

🏠 **Other:** praise, clapping, jumping up and down, cheering, petting gently, petting roughly, just hanging out together

These are just a taste of the reinforcements you can use to reward your dog. Be creative and watch your dog to see what he likes.

You might think that applying life rewards, rather than giving the dog a piece of food, will slow down training. True, the session may take a bit longer, but in the long run, the behaviors trained will be learned faster, stay longer, and be stronger.

Pack Your Bags—We're Going to Hawaii!: Adding Surprise Elements

Do you want to be a great trainer? There's a method to the madness and you need to do very real planning to become a great teacher. While it may seem to be difficult at first, it becomes simple with practice. It can end up being a way of life for many people because the benefits to the dog and your relationship are enormous and obvious.

What's more yummy? A plain banana, or a banana with three kinds of your favorite ice cream, plus hot fudge and chocolate sprinkles? Or how would you feel about packing for your vacation that you think will be to Colonial Williamsburg and your spouse surprises you with tickets to Hawaii?

Which do you think would be more fun for your dog? Eating the same old dry biscuit ten times in a row for loose-leash walking, or getting one piece of tortellini, a scratch behind the ears, the chance to chase you, five pieces of hot dog, a short game of tug, and a belly rub for the same loose-leash walking?

The point is to be unpredictable, *plan* surprise rewards, be generous, be fun, be variable in how and when and how much you reinforce, and you'll have the trained dog of your dreams.

Pooch Pointers _____

Using the methods in this book, you can go from being a lousy trainer to being a great one. Great trainers do the following:

- 🏠 Are good at reinforcing.
- 🏠 Are quick and have good timing.
- 🏠 Are generous and use lots of reinforcements.
- 🏠 Are unpredictable and vary when, how much, and how they apply reinforcers.
- 🏠 Are variable and use many different types of reinforcers.
- 🏠 Stop problems before they become locked in as solid behaviors.
- 🏠 Plan out their sessions carefully.
- 🏠 Recognize small approximations and reward them.
- 🏠 Keep a log or diary of each behavior being taught.

The Least You Need to Know

- 🏠 Fixed schedules of reinforcement kill behaviors.

- 🏠 Variable schedules of reinforcement create stronger behaviors and make training more fun and rewarding for your dog.

- 🏠 Plan surprise rewards for your dog.

- 🏠 Design a game strategy to become a great trainer.

Part  Let the Games Begin! Positive Training in Action

Okay, on to the nitty-gritty! Let's get started on socialization, eye contact, name recognition, "Come," "Sit," "Down," loose-leash walking, and all the other things that drive us as dog owners crazy. I've broken down the training for each of these behaviors (and more) into tiny steps for you to follow. Go slowly and patiently and refer to this book while you're actually training. You'll be amazed at how quickly your dog will catch on!

Chapter 10

The Most Important Things You and Your Dog Need to Know

In This Chapter

- Start with a good relationship
- Things you must do before you start training
- Teach your dog to stare at you adoringly
- Come to me, baby!

Before you start training in earnest, there are certain things you and your dog must master together. This chapter discusses the importance of building a relationship with your dog before you start asking him to learn the behaviors you want. Once you've done that, you can work toward starting your training sessions by teaching eye contact and priming the clicker. Then you can teach your dog the all-important "Come" command.

Let's Go to the Movies: Build Your Relationship

To get the behaviors you want and need from your dog, you must build a relationship first. In fact, 99 percent of all dog training is building your relationship and learning to read your dog (as discussed in Chapter 7). The other 1 percent is the actual obedience and manners stuff. Try to get the manners without the relationship and you won't succeed.

Just Say No to "No"

The first step to building a relationship with your dog is to stop all negativity. Drop all physical and verbal punishments, including the word *"No."* *"No"* very easily escalates into a screamed *"No!"* which dredges up some very negative emotion from us, which is then transmitted to the dog. Remember—associative learning happens 24 hours a day, 7 days a week, whether you want it to or not. You just can't get away from Pavlov!

Doggie Data _____

Positive training might very well change *your* life as well as your dog's. Sally and John brought their Golden Retriever pup for training. After six weeks of diligently practicing each week, they told me they actually stopped saying "No" to *each other!* Another client, Henry, was a very sullen, negative person with job-related problems and two very nice mixed-breed puppies. After training with me for a few weeks, he mentioned that positively training his dogs had turned his life around. He started to treat his co-workers in a more positive manner and was doing a better job at work. The best part is that everyone on the job noticed and complimented him on his change of attitude.

Look at it this way. *"No"* is not a verb. It doesn't tell the dog what you want him to do *instead* of what he is doing at the moment. *"No"* does nothing positive for the relationship between you and your dog. Imagine living with someone who was always nitpicking, screaming at you, hitting you—not the makings of a match made in heaven. After awhile you may just give up because nothing you do is "right." Same with your dog. Focus on what he's doing right and you'll all be happier.

Other "bad" words to stay away from: *"Eh-eh," "Oops," "Wrong," "Phooey"*—and any other words you come up with to mean *"No." "No"* is counterproductive and you'll get better behaviors faster without it.

Doggie Data

There aren't really any "good" or "bad" behaviors—there are just behaviors. Good and bad are subjective. I allow my dogs on the furniture, so for me, getting on the furniture is a "good" behavior. Other people may dislike having their dogs on the furniture, so for them, getting on the furniture is a "bad" behavior.

Pooch Pointers

There are three magic words to use instead of "No"—"Come," "Sit," and "Give." Once your dog has learned what these behaviors mean (see Chapter 11), use them instead. If your dog has his paws up on the counter—"Come" works well. If your dog is digging through the garbage—"Come-Sit-Give" are the words you should use. I don't even use the words *"leave it,"* because that's too much like *"No." "Come"* works better because it gives the dog more direction.

Focus on the Good Stuff!

Too often we reinforce the dog by paying attention to him when he's doing something "bad" (such as eating the chair) and never notice the 23 hours a day he's actually doing good things. If we pay attention to the dog only when he's "bad," then he will do only "bad" things. We call this handler-induced "bad" behaviors (see Chapter 18). When he's laying down or being quiet or whatever you deem as appropriate behavior—*praise* him! If you can't watch him and you know he will soon be driving you crazy, just put him in his crate before he starts practicing any "bad" behaviors.

> **Canine Caveats**
>
> Putting the dog in his crate should not be used as a punishment. You can even throw in a toy or a treat, so the crate isn't seen as a punishment. Putting the dog away *after* a bad behavior has happened does not teach the dog anything. However, it keeps you from killing the dog! Next time, watch his signals more closely and put him away *before* he gets out of control.

Communing with Nature

Don't underestimate the value of just taking your dog to a park, sitting on a park bench, and just hangin' out. On very hot days or days I'm just feeling lazy, I'll pack up the dogs in the van, go someplace pretty, green, and shady, and just hang out with each dog, one at a time. That way, they all get some "alone" time with me.

I add massage along with petting and we watch the world go by, as I thank my lucky stars I am working at a job that allows me to do this! Any fun or relaxing thing you share with your dog builds up some nice money in the bank account of your relationship.

Get Started with Training

Before any training can start, your dog needs to know a few things. You need to make the click sound valuable and meaningful, and you need to teach him that eye contact with you, and hearing his name and "Come," are worth a million bucks. You cannot train a dog if he is not focused on you. Well, you can, but then you'd be using choke, prong, and shock collars, and that is not why you bought this book!

First Things First

First of all, start your session by priming the clicker to remind your dog that "click" means food. Have a handful of treats ready and the dog in front of you, and follow these steps:

1. Click the clicker.

2. Hand your dog one treat within one-half second after the click (this is the optimum timing—after 3 seconds the dog won't make the proper association that click means food).

3. Repeat for at least two minutes.

You shouldn't have to do this more than two minutes. If your dog doesn't make the connection right away, don't think you have a lemon—just do it longer.

Look into My Eyes: Eye Contact

In the same training session, (after priming the clicker) you are now going to teach the dog to stare at you adoringly. Without eye contact, you can't teach the dog anything, so logistically, this is the next step in training.

Again, have a handful of treats ready and the dog in front of you. Now follow these steps:

1. Wait for eye contact. Your dog will probably mug your hand, so if needed, put your hands behind your back. Keep your eyes on your dog and just wait silently.

2. Be ready to click and treat. Usually after three to ten seconds, your dog will accidentally look up at your face.

3. Stand still and wait again. The next time your dog looks at you, click and treat. On average, it takes dogs two to three minutes to figure out where the "magic button" is (looking at your face).

Repeat for a minute or two every day for two weeks and then a few times a week for the rest of the dog's life.

(Photo by P. Dennison)

Making eye contact.

My Name Is "No, No Bad Dog!"—What's Yours?

Does your dog know his name? Or if he does, does he think hearing his name is a bad thing? The fastest, easiest, most surefire way to teach your dog that his name is valuable and something to respond to instantly, is this (again, borrowing from Pavlov—name means reinforcement):

1. Have a few treats in your hand or pocket.

2. When the dog gives you eye contact, say his name.

3. Then click and treat.

Repeat for five to ten minutes every day for two weeks and then a few times a week for the rest of the dog's life.

In the beginning stages, be sure you don't use the dog's name to get him to look at you—say his name *after* he looks at you. After a day or two, you should start to see the dog get whiplash looking at you when you say his name.

Canine Caveats

You can very easily train your dog to ignore his name. Say your dog is out in the yard and you want him in the house. You call his name. He ignores you. You continue to call his name repeatedly. Each time you yell it louder and louder and louder, hoping that if you scream his name at the top of your lungs, he will finally answer you. Guess what? He won't, and now he'll ignore his name whenever you use it. You can even do this with "Come" as well! Yippee!

In the beginning stages, if you can't get your dog to respond, whoop and holler in glee and run the other way. Ninety-nine percent of dogs will run after you. Chasing the dog will only drive him farther away from you. Until you have a strong name response and "Come" cue, don't let the dog off the leash.

To continue to keep eye contact strong, every time you say the dog's name and he responds, reinforce him! "Good! You responded when I said your name! Brilliant doggie!" Be sure to heavily reinforce, especially when there are distractions around—then really go crazy and make him think he won a million dollars at a slot machine.

Dogs Don't Naturally Know What "Good Dog" Means

To drive up the value of your praise words (remember, these words are not naturally reinforcing for your dog), pair them with food. You don't have to click for this one. You're turning your praise words into a marker signal—just as you did with the clicker.

To make your words into reinforcements, follow the preceding steps for priming the clicker. Say your praise word(s): "Good dog," "Wahoo," "Yippee," "Excellent," and so on and then treat within one-half second. If you use many different ones (as I do), say one word per session.

Pooch Pointers

You can even make your smile into a marker signal. I do this because I can't bring food into the obedience ring, so I use a smile as a reward. If the judges ever make us wear paper bags over our heads during competition, I'm in big trouble.

Because we talk to and around our dogs, and dogs are not a verbal species, speech tends to become white noise to them. You need to do this exercise for more than two minutes (as we did with the clicker). Continue to pair the praise word with food a few times per day for a few weeks.

I'd Rather Eat Poop: "Come"

The most important thing you can teach your dog is to come reliably when called (also known as a *recall*). This behavior could save his life one day, so please don't skimp on your training of it. The first step to building a reliable "Come" is to continue to build your relationship, and be variable and unpredictable in how you reinforce his behavior.

The hardest thing that we're up against is learning to become "more interesting than spit on the sidewalk." It takes creativity, patience, perseverance, and management. If your dog doesn't have a reliable recall, don't let him off the leash in an unprotected area.

Step One: Use Associative Learning

Start training your dog to come with these steps:

1. Have a few treats in your hand or pocket and have the dog in front of you.

2. When the dog gives you eye contact, say his name, then "Come."

3. Click and treat.

4. Repeat for a minute or two (20 times) every day for two weeks and then a few times a week for the rest of the dog's life.

In this session, you don't expect the dog to actually move out of position. You just want him to listen to the words. If your dog has a history of ignoring the word "Come," feel free to change your word. "Here" is a popular recall word.

Recall the "basic recipe":

- For this behavior alone, do not phase out the food or other reinforcers—*ever*—for the life of the dog. Reinforcers can be petting, praise, food, a rousing game of tug. Whatever the dog loves, do them all!

- Make your "Come" signal distinct (not sometimes, "C'mere," sometimes "Come," sometimes, "Here," sometimes "Let's Go," and so on). In the beginning stages of the recall, don't say the word unless your dog is already on his way to you! You *must* pair the word with the behavior for the dog to learn exactly what "Come" means.

- Say "Come" only when you're prepared to reinforce heavily— for at least 20 seconds! If you don't have anything on you, you can run to the reinforcers, all the while keeping his attention on you.

- Make sure the dog comes within a few inches—do not reach out to feed the dog.

- Make sure that when you say "Come" it doesn't sound like this: "Comecomecomecome-come." To the dog's ear that sounds different from "Come," so your cue will be confusing.

Canine Caveats

Be sure to use the word "Come" *only* for a recall. Don't dilute it by using it for loose-leash walking or anything else.

126 **Part 3:** Let the Games Begin! Positive Training in Action

Step Two: Play Hide-and-Seek

Have someone hold your dog while you run away and hide. Then call the dog. The instant you say the dog's name ("Fluffy, Come"), your helper should drop the leash. When the dog finds you, have a huge party with all sorts of reinforcers.

(Photo by P. Dennison)

A person dropping the leash as the owner calls the dog.

Or if you're alone, just run and hide while the dog is in another room, and then call him. I do this with my dogs—it's pretty funny with four dogs in a teeny tiny house all skidding around trying to get to me first.

Step Three: Wounded Caribou

This is also called the "rev up and cool down game," and I use it for puppies or adolescent dogs that do a lot of jumping or biting when aroused. This is how it works:

1. Run a few steps. (The dog will chase you because that's what dogs like to do most.)

2. After a few steps—before the dog gets too aroused—stop running and walk really sl-o-o-w-ly and don't look at the dog whatsoever. Keep moving slowly until the dog also slows down. After a few steps of peace and calm, click and treat the dog.

3. Repeat steps one and two. You'll see the dog slow down sooner each time.

4. You can also throw in some "Sits" and "Downs" or any other behavior your dog may already know before you reinforce him.

This game teaches the dog to settle down without jumping or nipping by using the dog's own language—moving slowly and turning away.

Step Four: Walking in a Field or Trail

Bring your fanny pack, some toys and treats, and a long leash. *Before* the dog gets to the end of the line, say his name. You don't want his name associated with a painful pop on the collar, which is why you do it before he hits the end of the leash.

If he responds by turning his head to you, say "Come." When he comes to you, click once and treat heavily. You can even run backwards, enticing him to come to you. (Be sure you don't yank him by the collar.) Continue to practice this as you continue your walk. If he doesn't respond to his name, don't say it again right now. Wait until you really think he will respond— this would not be when his entire head is down in a gopher hole.

Pooch Pointers
If your dog doesn't respond, just stand still and wait. If needed, turn your back to the dog and wait. You can even try squatting down. He'll eventually come to you, and when he does, click once and reward heavily with all types of reinforcers.

128 **Part 3:** Let the Games Begin! Positive Training in Action

Step Five: Drop the Cookie and Run Like Heck Game

This is a wonderful "Come" game that both you and the dog will love. And you get to continue to build that positive relationship because all of these training exercises are *fun!* Follow these steps:

1. Throw a cookie a few feet away. (Make sure the dog sees it!)

2. Tell your dog to "Get It."

3. Run away fast!

4. As the dog is coming to you, say "Come" (pairing the word with the behavior).

5. When he gets to you, you click and treat with a *jackpot.* Jackpots are given *for every "Come" and are fed one cookie at a time.* To a dog, a wad of food is the same as one cookie, so spread them out and keep the dog with you longer! Be variable in the number of cookies in the jackpots. Add in lots of play, petting, and praise as reinforcers.

Muttley Meanings
A **jackpot** is lots of treats given to the dog all one at a time. I like to give a jackpot when the dog has done something hard for the very first time or if a behavior is particularly wonderful.

Doggie Data
You don't want the dog to get used to taking one cookie and then running away from you because he knows you pay out only one cookie. One day he'll be distracted by something more interesting than your one cookie, such as a squirrel. Chasing that squirrel could lead him into the path of a truck.

You can also do this exercise without running. Just throw the treat farther away and wait for the dog to get it. Once he finds the treat, call him to you. You want to vary this with running away because otherwise your dog will think the recall signal is you running away.

This is a *super* game to play with all family members in a big circle—kind of a "round robin" game. The dogs love it, the kids love it, and the dogs get really tired. And everyone knows that a tired dog is a good dog!

(Photo by C. Palmer)

Dropping the cookie …

(Photo by C. Palmer)

… and running like heck (and calling your dog to "Come" as he is coming).

Step Six: Adding Distractions

Get yourself a 50-foot long line and practice, in tons of locations where there are distractions, all of the "Come" behaviors we just described. The long line becomes a portable fence! You can't exercise a dog properly on a six-foot leash, and I don't use leashes as "tools." Leashes are to be used as safety nets only.

The heavier the distractions, the larger and more exciting your reinforcers should be. Start with small distractions that are far away and gradually build to greater ones that are closer.

You can practice this method with many distractions—not all of course. You don't want to allow your dog to chase cars, but you can still train an instant recall for when he's aroused by using "safe" and highly valued distractions. Although your dog loves to chase cars, he also loves to chase balls or Frisbees, so you can use his high arousal to toys (instead of speeding cars) to train for instant recall. Teach your dog to come off a toy in the midst of chasing it by following these steps:

1. Have the dog off leash in a safe area or on a 50-foot long line with it dragging. Start off with the very lowest valued item you can think of, such as a paper-towel tube.

2. Throw the tube.

3. Tell the dog to "Get It."

4. As the dog goes toward it—just a step or two—call him back to you and heavily reward him with toys he likes, petting, praise, or food.

5. Throw the tube again and repeat a few times until the dog is running back to you at top speed.

6. Now find another item, slightly more valued than the tube. Repeat the exercise, always rewarding heavily for the recall. Gradually increase the value of the thrown toy while increasing the value of your rewards when he does come back to you.

7. If at any point your dog ignores you and ends up getting the toy, don't say anything—just stand there passively, count to five, and just start over. Don't block the dog or become a barrier.

(Photo by J. Guz)

A Border Collie coming away from a tennis ball.

This is not about "obedience" (how *dare* he not come back to me?); this is about building your relationship, so that your dog *wants* to play this game with you, and *wants* to come off a toy, bike, car, deer, because playing with you is *fun* to do.

Continue in short sessions—three to five throws of the object per session—until you're using the highest valued toy imaginable and your dog is making skid marks in the grass to come back to you. Periodically, allow him to get to the toy without calling him back to you, play with him with the toy, and then work your recall again. The more practice you can do with your recalls with safe objects when the dog is aroused, the more easily he will come off inappropriate objects when in that same state.

The Least You Need to Know

- The basis of good training is first building a positive relationship with your dog.

- Before you can start training, you must prime the clicker, master eye contact and name recognition, and build praise word recognition.

- Teaching your dog to come when called is important in later training and could one day save his life.

- Have fun with your dog—continue to add to the piggy bank of your relationship.

Chapter 11

Positive Puppy Socialization

In This Chapter

🏠 Hello, world—socialization basics

🏠 Getting your dog used to being touched

🏠 Do I know you?

🏠 It's a big, scary world out there

Puppies are like little sponges—they soak up whatever you teach them. It's your job to make sure all of those early associations are good ones. I've worked with many eight-week-old puppies and they very rapidly learn proper behaviors without the use of punishment.

This chapter is devoted to socialization and the things you need to do to make sure your puppy grows into a confident adult. If you don't have time to do these things for your puppy, you might want to rethink owning a dog. It's your responsibility to "bring up baby" correctly and humanely. If you practice socialization—getting your dog accustomed to petting, handling, meeting strangers, and being polite around food and the food bowl—you and your dog will live "happily ever after."

These methods are also great when working with rescued dogs. If you've started out using punishment-based methods and want to switch to positive, never fear! Dogs are resilient and you can turn them around.

Social(ization) Studies

The optimum time for socialization is 8 weeks to 20 weeks. Any time after that you'll be dealing with *counterconditioning* and *desensitization* because you've lost your window of opportunity.

Muttley Meanings

Counterconditioning is the use of associative learning to reverse the unwanted effects of prior conditioning. **Desensitization,** or systematic desensitization, is a form of counterconditioning; it's a procedure in which a phobic subject (human or animal) is subjected to low levels of the frightening stimulus while relaxed. The level of frightening stimulus is gradually increased, but never at a rate to cause distress. Eventually the fear dissipates.

Everyone says that you should "properly socialize" your new pup, but no one tells you exactly how to go about it. Because *socialization* is so vitally important to your dog's future mental and emotional well-being and outlook on life, it's imperative to start your new pup off on the right paw.

Muttley Meanings

Socialization involves the controlled introduction of various situations and things so that the dog develops positive associations with them.

Some people may think that socializing a dog means indiscriminately dragging him around to new locations or having strangers walk up and invasively pet him. This method of socialization may very well lead to behavior problems later, such as fear or aggression. Proper socialization is actually a controlled introduction of various situations and things so that the dog develops positive associations with them.

(Photo by P. Dennison)

Bull Mastiff puppy with a dumbbell.

Socialization is about exposing your puppy gradually and systematically to different types of people, places, things, surfaces, noises, touch (from you and strangers), other dogs, and other species of animals. Socialization is all about setting the dog up for success—introducing him to each new situation in such a manner that he won't be afraid. The goal is to build confidence and trust.

Socialization Can Be Stressful

The most important aspect of training is the detection of signs of stress and fear in your puppy. If you don't recognize these signs, you may be pushing the dog into a situation that he can't deal with and may be creating more fear, aggression, or anxiety about a specific place/person/species. (See Chapters 7 and 8 for the observable signs of stress.)

If your dog exhibits any of these signs, this may be an indicator that you have pushed your socialization session too fast or for too long.

Places for Socialization

What will your dog have to feel comfortable with during his lifetime? He'll visit the veterinarian and groomer, where he will be handled by strangers in sometimes very uncomfortable ways. You'll want to take your dog to the park, new and different places, and in and out of strange doorways. You'll also want him to be comfortable going to the kennel. He'll also need to feel comfortable with strangers coming into your house.

 Pooch Pointers

There will come a time when you'll need to board your dog (at a reputable kennel, please—get many references and check them out). Don't wait until you're actually going on vacation to teach the dog to like the kennel. Start by leaving him for an hour with yummy treats and plenty of chew toys. Repeat many times, gradually increasing the time he stays in the kennel. If an hour is too much for your pup, start at five minutes and slowly build the duration of time he can be without you comfortably. If the kennel won't allow you to do this without charge, it's not a kennel you would want to use, anyway.

The dog will need to feel comfortable walking on different types of surfaces such as concrete, gravel, linoleum, carpet, wood or tile floors, grass, snow, puddles, mud, and ice. You need to build his confidence in going up and down all different types of stairs, jumping into the car on his own (especially useful if you have a large-breed dog), riding in the car, and walking along a busy street. Your dog needs to get used to seeing or hearing men in hats or with beards, people in wheelchairs, kids on skateboards, umbrellas, babies crying, kids playing, bicycles, loud music and other sounds, cars driving by, other dogs—the list is endless!

Cuddle Time: Petting and Handling

Repetition of calm behaviors is one of the building blocks to a healthy and happy relationship with your dog.

It's a dangerous world out there and it's important to recognize that uninvited hands or faces reaching down toward a dog's head are seen, from the dog's perspective, as being aggressive. As a consequence, a large percentage of dog bites happen to children because children enthusiastically push themselves abruptly into a dog's face. You don't have to just "put up with" your dog's dislike of handling—you can *train* him to love it.

Canine Caveats
We have all experienced children and adults coming up to our dogs and wanting to pet them. In this litigious society, it's important to get in touch with your pet's state of mind when you expose him to others. It's also important to teach strangers the correct way to approach your dog.

Here's That Word Again: Desensitization

You think your dog needs to be bathed and brushed and he thinks otherwise. He bites you or the brush, or he may not even let you get that far—he may run away at the sight of anything that even looks like a grooming implement. And toenail clipping? Forget about it!

The first step to teaching your dog how to handle unwanted attention with a minimum of stress is to begin the process of desensitization. An additional side benefit is that as you "work" with your dog in this way, you build a level of trust and establish a kind of communication that makes your training with him easier as you move into more advanced levels. Before starting these sessions, you must first practice the behaviors (priming the clicker, "Sit," "Down," "Stand," and eye contact) in Chapters 10 and 12.

Training Your Dog to Accept Touching

The goal of this exercise is to reinforce *no movement* from the dog while you touch him. Start your session by giving your dog a few treats to get his attention. Break the training session into two to three sessions of approximately five minutes each. Keep your sessions short and successful—just a few minutes at a time, as many times per day as you can fit in. Be sure to include all family members in the touching sessions—not all at once, but one at a time.

Position your body so that you're facing in the same direction as your dog. This is usually seen as nonthreatening and may actually be calming to your dog.

Try not to lean over him. Some dogs may experience leaning over as dominant, intimidating, aggressive, or scary. Possible reactions to this are backing away, jumping up to your face, lowering of his head in submission, or in extreme cases, biting.

(Photo by P. Dennison)

A person facing the same way as the dog.

(Photo by P. Dennison)

A person leaning over a puppy and the puppy displaying a submissive reaction.

Now follow these "basic recipe" steps:

1. Have a treat in one hand and hold it out about 12 to 30 inches from your dog's face. You don't want to tease the dog—just get his focus on the treat.

2. Place your other hand along the dog's neck—not petting, just a soft touch.

(Photo by P. Dennison)

A person holding a treat at the proper distance while touching the dog.

3. If the dog doesn't move, click and give him a treat. At the same time, remove your other hand from his neck. (Have the clicker and treat in the same hand—don't try to pet with food in your hand.)

4. If the dog does move, stop what you're doing and just start again.

5. Repeat about 10 times or until the dog is feeling comfortable and is consistently not moving.

(Photo by P. Dennison)

The correct way to hold the clicker and food in one hand.

For the very young pup, you can slather some kind of nut butter (*not* peanut butter; it's toxic to your dog) on the refrigerator and let him lick it while you gently brush or pet with a light stroke. Stop before he's done licking. You can do this in the bathtub as well. Get him used to all different kinds of things as early as possible.

Using the five steps of the "basic recipe" listed previously, continue to do these exercises. Place your hand gently along the side of the dog's face. Once he's comfortable with that, you can add in head touching and then slowly add in each body part: ears, tail, face, back of his neck and shoulders, each leg, foot, and toe, gums and teeth. Keep your sessions short and successful—just a few minutes at a time, as many times a day as you can fit in.

Pooch Pointers

If you feel all thumbs, have someone help you. One of you can click for no movement and the other person can touch and then feed once he or she hears the click.

(Photo by P. Dennison)

Owner leaning over the dog while distracting him with food.

Repeat these exercises a few times per day for a few weeks, touching all body parts gently. Once he likes gentle petting, you can gradually add rougher petting. You can even teach the dog to accept pinching (which is a similar sensation to getting an injection), by using this method.

Pooch Pointers

When picking up feet, especially a back one, remember that dogs don't naturally know how to stand on three legs. Place your other hand gently under his belly to give him some support. Once the pup gets the hang of it, you won't need to help him keep from falling over.

Be careful and go slowly. If you let go, you are reinforcing the struggling. If you don't let go, you may freak him out. The best course is to go slowly enough so that the dog *likes* being handled. Redirect with a treat if needed. The key here is to slowly build up to complete body touching so that the dog wouldn't even think about moving away.

(Photo by P. Dennison)

Supporting the dog to keep his balance while holding his back leg up.

This may take quite a few sessions depending on how sensitive your pup is to handling. Don't rush and don't get angry—these emotions will get you in trouble later.

If you decide you want to clip your dog's nails yourself, just cut off the tip of them at first. If you're nervous at all—just one iota of nervousness, do not, I repeat, *do not* clip your dog's nails. All it takes it one "Oh my god, I made you bleed," while you run around screaming hysterically, to turn your dog into a toenail demon. You can still teach the dog to accept this and leave the actual clipping to a professional.

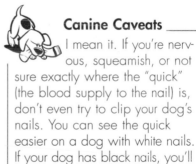

Canine Caveats

I mean it. If you're nervous, squeamish, or not sure exactly where the "quick" (the blood supply to the nail) is, don't even try to clip your dog's nails. You can see the quick easier on a dog with white nails. If your dog has black nails, you'll be working blind.

Stranger Danger

Progressing on to the next stage, acclimating the dog to strangers, you start by allowing your dog to observe strangers from a distance. Later you let him get closer to people and have them touch him.

From a Distance

Go to a place where there are just a few people and few distractions, staying approximately 50 to 100 feet away. As the dog continues to remain calm, you can gradually go in closer.

If your dog is frightened and tries to back up or run away, *do not* say "It's okay, it's okay!" or console him in any way. Consoling a dog reinforces the dog's fear because dogs don't speak English (really!). No matter what you say, you're still paying attention to the dog and rewarding the fearful behavior. The best course is to …

1. Say *nothing!* Do nothing.

2. Stand there passively and keep your eyes on your dog.

3. Once his body relaxes, praise him, then ask him to do whatever he knows how to do ("Sit," "Down") and then keep him busy interacting with you.

Canine Caveats

It's easy to get caught in the trap of thinking that if your dog is frantically wagging his tail, he's deliriously happy. A frantically wagging tail is just that—frantic. (Yes, even if your puppy is a Lab.) It's a typical puppy submissive behavior, showing stress. It's one way a subordinate puppy approaches an adult dog. He's saying "Please don't kill me, I am so cute!"

Timing is everything—note that the praise and rewards come *after* the dog is calm and then performs another behavior. If you gave the dog rewards when the dog was nervous, you'd be reinforcing the nervousness.

If the dog is frightened and growls, lunges, or barks, *do not* verbally or physically reprimand the dog. Why? By punishing the dog, he'll make the association that when people are around, bad things happen. Do this enough and the dog will become a fearful, aggressive dog that will bite people in the future. The way to handle this type of fear display is exactly the same as in the preceding example.

Keep your sessions short—just a few minutes each time. Go to as many different locations as you can, as often as you can, and do the same exercise, rewarding heavily for calm, focused attention to you.

Pooch Pointers

Gentle stroking calms a dog; vigorous petting energizes a dog. You want calm behaviors here, so gentle is the way to go.

First Contact

When your dog is comfortable just watching people, then you can invite some strangers to come up and pet him. My favorite way is to feed my dog treats while the stranger is petting. That way, positive associations are happening while strangers approach (there's Pavlov again!). If John Q. Public starts to stress your dog out, you can just lure him away with a treat at the earliest signs of stress you see. If you've done your homework, your dog won't be nervous when strangers lean over him.

Don't know where to go to try this out? Try the vet's office, the groomer (make sure to get permission and go at a time of day that isn't hectic and overcrowded with people and dogs), the park, a school yard, fields, parking lots, even the bank—some of them allow well-mannered dogs. Be creative!

Canine Caveats

Please don't skimp or try to rush ahead with these exercises. Your patience will be rewarded.

(Photo by P. Dennison)

An owner feeding a puppy while a stranger approaches.

Properly desensitizing your puppy to all sorts of handling takes a little effort in the beginning, but it will pay off in the end. Do your job right and you won't have a dog that needs to be sedated for grooming or toenail clipping.

It's a Wild, Wild, Wild World: The Environment

When introducing your dog to "stuff," be sure to do it gradually. After all, drainpipes may be out to murder you! The best way to handle introductions is to be passive and ignore all but calm reactions to things. If the dog is terrified of a piece of paper, don't laugh, don't comfort, and don't scold. Just stand there quietly—you can laugh hysterically later—and then reinforce calm behavior.

Go through your list of "things my dog needs to get used to," systematically and carefully and you will have a nice, well-grounded puppy that grows up into a nice, well-adjusted adult.

Food

You *must*, I repeat *must* teach your dog to be calm around food—his and yours. You don't want your adorable puppy ending up ripping off some kid's face because he wants the kid's cookie, or growling and snapping as your child passes by your dog's food bowl as he's eating.

I'm *not* saying you should forcibly take things out of your dog's mouth—that will only *teach* him that he *needs* to guard food and toys because you're going to take things away from him. There are simple ways of teaching him that giving up food and objects is to his benefit. Follow these steps:

1. Have the dog in a "Stay."

2. Drop a piece of food on the floor while reminding the dog to "Stay."

3. If he "Stays" for even a second at first, click and then *take the treat to him*, reinforcing the "Stay."

4. If the dog breaks position at any time, say nothing; just step on the food (if you're fast enough). If you aren't fast enough, just try again.

5. Continue to do steps 1 to 3, having him "Stay" for longer periods of time before taking the treat to him.

Pooch Pointers
Taking the treat to him is vital—you don't want him to forage for food, and you want to reinforce the "Stay" position.

Once the dog is doing well with one piece of food, add a few more until you can drop wads of food on the ground while he continues to "Stay" and give you eye contact.

The next step is calling the dog away from dropped food:

1. Drop food on the floor. (Don't drop it where the dog has to pass it to get to you.)

2. Move away from the food and your dog.

3. Call the dog.

4. Heavily reinforce the dog for coming to you with 10 times the amount of food he left behind.

You can even run away while calling, or I'll allow you to cheat the first few times and use squeaky toys to help the dog be successful. If the dog isn't successful, don't worry about it—no reprimands, no body blocking (putting your body between the dog and the food), just try again.

Doggie Food Bowls

If you don't train your dog to be calm around food bowls, you may be asking for food-guarding issues later on. Skip these exercises and you'd better fill up your first aid kit! Follow these steps:

1. Hand your dog a bowl with a few pieces of food in it.

2. When he's done eating, take the bowl away and give him another one with a few pieces of food in it.

3. Repeat bunches of times—15 to 20 times.

Now comes the second step:

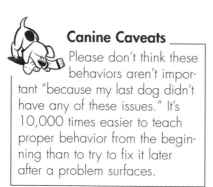

Canine Caveats

Please don't think these behaviors aren't important "because my last dog didn't have any of these issues." It's 10,000 times easier to teach proper behavior from the beginning than to try to fix it later after a problem surfaces.

1. Hand your dog a bowl with a few pieces of food in it.

2. Before he's done eating, lower your hand to the bowl and add more food to it.

3. Repeat bunches of times— 20 to 25 times over the course of a few days.

Now for the third step with the food bowl:

1. Hand your dog a bowl with a few pieces of food in it.

2. Before he's done eating, gently remove the food bowl *at the exact same time that you hand him another bowl with a few pieces of food in it.*

3. Repeat these steps 30 to 50 times over the course of a few days.

Make it *fun* for your dog—make it *more* reinforcing when you take the food bowl away than when he keeps it to himself. You can always add more food in the second bowl than you did in the first bowl.

Other Dogs

Go to school! Numerous times! I mean it! The average puppy kindergarten lasts from six to eight weeks. Don't expect your puppy to be thoroughly "socialized" with other dogs for the rest of his life in such a short time. Start your own puppy playgroup and keep it going. Put up flyers at the vet's office, pet shops, or groomer asking other people to bring their pups to your playgroup.

Even if you have other dogs at home and your puppy gets along fine, don't think this is enough. Your new puppy needs to be exposed to many other dogs in his lifetime. Be sure, however, that the puppies and older dogs you introduce him to are friendly. It would be terrible to have your puppy attacked and possibly traumatized for life, ending up fearful of his own species.

Doing these exercises *from the day you bring the dog home* may save you a great deal of heartache later. Continue to periodically practice all of these behaviors for the life of the dog.

Canine Caveats _____

As your puppy gets older, he might develop new fears. One day he'll be fine with something and the next day he'll be terrified. These are called *fear periods*.

The typical ages for fear periods are 8 to 10 weeks of age, then 16 to 20 weeks, then approximately 6 months, and yet again around 10 months. Fear periods taper off and return out of the blue around 14 to 18 months. Fear periods can occur even as late as three or four years.

It's *vital* that you don't laugh at, scold, or comfort the dog during fear periods. Ignore and wait for calm behaviors that you can then reinforce. If you pressure a puppy during a fear period, he will have that fear for life.

The Least You Need to Know

- Socialization is a controlled introduction of various situations and things so that the dog develops positive associations with them.

- Work on the basics from the day you get your pup: petting, handling, people food, and food bowls.

- Be sure to watch for any signs of stress, stop training, and rethink your next session.

- One puppy kindergarten does not make a well socialized dog—continue training!

Chapter 12

The Basics, Plus Settle, Rollover, and Door Etiquette

In This Chapter

-  Please be seated
- Take a load off and lie down
- Proper door protocol
- Settle down!

Sitting, lying down, and standing on command are extremely useful behaviors. You can use them as alternate behaviors to jumping, for proper greeting behaviors, for veterinarian visits, and even to counter aggression, and they're the basis for many other behaviors. The great thing is that they're all very easy to teach and there's very little your dog can do wrong when he's sitting or lying down. This chapter also discusses how to teach your dog to behave when he's near an open door.

Puppy Pushups: "Sit," "Down," and "Stand"

The key to teaching the basic behaviors in this section is to associate the correct word with the behavior you want. Your dog is running around the yard and you call him to "Come." He doesn't know the meaning of the word, and yet you keep calling him anyway. He is running around, playing with a toy, urinating, barking, and digging, while you scream "Come!" The next time you say "Come," he will say to you, "I know what that means!" and run around, play with a toy, urinate, bark, and dig. Why? Because those were the behaviors you paired with the word "Come."

Canine Caveats

When teaching any behavior, it's vital that you don't say the word before the behavior happens. It's imperative that you add the word for the behavior at precisely the correct time. If you say the word "Sit" while the dog is standing, then what behavior have you named "Sit"? The stand!

"Sit"

Get rid of the old "pull up on the leash and push down on the hind end" method of teaching a "Sit" and get ready for some fun:

1. Put a treat in your hand and hold your hand up over the dog's head (canine physics in action here—head goes up, butt goes down!). I recommend having your palm facing up for this signal.

2. Do *not* say "Sit" before the dog sits.

3. When his hind end hits the floor, say "Sit."

4. Then click and treat.

5. If the dog jumps up, simply take your hand away and try again, perhaps lowering your signal hand.

6. Repeat a few times with a treat in your hand.

7. Then take the treat out of your hand and continue to give your new hand signal (palm up).

8. For now, until the dog learns the behavior, continue to say the word "Sit" as the dog's hind end hits the ground.

(Photo by P. Dennison)

A dog sitting.

Canine Caveats

When you start to say the word before the behavior, be sure to say it only once. Don't get sucked into the trap of saying "Sit" repeatedly in the hope that the dog might finally understand. Saying the cue word repeatedly will only teach the dog to respond after the fiftieth "Sit."

Say your signal word and then wait for at least 10 seconds. You can say it one more time and wait again for 10 full seconds. If the dog still doesn't respond, go back to using the hand signal a few more times.

It's important to get the food out of your signal hand as soon as possible, because otherwise the dog is just following the treat. Usually you can start saying the word before the behavior after about a week or two.

"Down"

Now you can teach the "Down" in the same noninvasive way. You won't have to push down on your dog's shoulders or yank him down by the collar. This would only stress him out anyway, or at the very least, make him more resistant to lying down because you're activating his *opposition reflex*. Here's what to do:

1. Have a treat in your hand.

2. Ask the dog to "Sit."

3. Bring your hand (slowly) straight down to the ground.

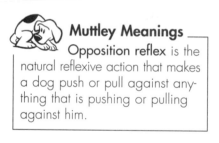

Muttley Meanings
Opposition reflex is the natural reflexive action that makes a dog push or pull against anything that is pushing or pulling against him.

4. When the dog lies down (not before), say "Down"; then click and treat.

5. Repeat a few times until the dog is lying down faster, and then take the food out of your signal hand, as you did with the "Sit."

If your dog doesn't lie down right away, make the steps smaller and use tiny approximations. Try this at first on a slippery floor rather than on carpeting.

1. When your dog lowers his head to follow your hand, click and treat.

2. When he lowers his head more, click and treat.

3. After a few repetitions, start to watch his shoulders. Hold your hand steady on the floor. As his shoulders start to lower, click and treat.

4. Continue in this vein and then click and treat when both shoulders are lowered.

5. Usually by this point, on the next try, your dog will lie down. Be sure to click and jackpot with lots of treats.

(Photo by P. Dennison)

A dog sitting and his owner starting to lure him into a "Down."

You should see the light bulb come on in your dog's eyes after a few more repetitions and he'll start to lie down faster and faster.

If your dog won't lie down using this method, don't think you have a stupid dog; he just doesn't understand what you want. You can try this:

1. Sit on the ground with your leg up, forming a "tent" with your knee. (If your dog is too big to go under your knee, you can use a chair or table rather than your knee.)

2. Have some treats in both hands.

3. Lure the dog under your knee.

4. Do *not* push the dog down with your leg.

5. Once the dog's shoulder is under your leg, slowly raise your hand with the treat so that his head follows. Usually he'll lie down at this point.

6. Be sure to say "Down" and then click and treat.

Repeat a bunch of times until the dog lies down fairly quickly. Now you'll have to fade out your knee:

1. Sit on the floor and don't raise your knee.

2. Move your hand in the same motion, as if you're luring your dog under your leg, but lure next to your leg.

3. When your dog lies down, say "Down," and click and treat.

Once the dog is lying down with a minimum lure from you, you can go back to the earlier steps and lure from a "Sit."

I'm sure you've been bending over or kneeling on the ground, so now is the time to start changing your cue to just a hand signal. Otherwise, you'll have to bend over for the rest of the dog's life. Here's what to do:

1. Ask the dog to "Sit."

2. Stand up straight and bring your signal hand down to the ground. Hold it there until the dog lies down. Then click and treat.

3. Repeat, but this time, bring your hand down to only about two inches off the ground and hold it there. Your dog will probably look at you in confusion, but hold your position. He may also mug your hand. Just stay still. He will lie down. Click and treat when he does.

4. The next step is to bend over so that your hand is now about four inches from the ground. Wait again until your dog lies down. Click and treat when he does.

5. Continue along in this vein until you're standing straight and just doing a simple hand motion without bending over. Be sure to stand up straighter only about two inches at a time.

(Photo by P. Dennison)

A handler standing straight up, using a hand signal to tell the dog to go "Down."

Do the these steps over a few days. Don't forget: Too much drilling can be seen as a form of punishment by the dog.

As with the "Sit," be sure to continue to say the word "Down" as the dog is lying down, not before. It usually takes about two weeks for the dog to learn the behavior reliably. At that time you can then start to say the word "Down" before the behavior.

Canine Caveats

You may start to notice that your dog responds better to your hand signal than to your verbal signal. Your dog isn't stupid. Dogs are more in tune with their physical environment, which includes our body language. Learning what our spoken words mean is harder for them to figure out than what our hand signals mean.

When practicing the "Sits" and "Downs," try not to always do them in the same order. Dogs notice patterns. You may think the dog knows the behavior, but he doesn't—he only knows the order in which the behaviors are performed. If you always ask for a "Sit" and then a "Down," and now you ask for a "Down" from a "Stand," your dog may look at you blankly. You don't have a stupid dog, you just pattern trained him. So mix it up and keep him guessing and interested.

"Stand"

Stand is useful for grooming, nail clipping, and vet visits. And if you want to compete with your dog at shows, "Stand" is a must. Here's how to teach him:

1. Have your dog in a "Sit" position on your left side.

2. Put your right hand in front of the dog's nose and slowly lure him, with a treat in your flat hand, into the standing position.

3. Be sure not to say "Stand" until he does the behavior. As soon as he stands, say "Stand," then click and treat.

(Photo by P. Dennison)

Holding the treat properly when luring into the "Stand."

(Photo by P. Dennison)

Dog on left of handler. Handler using right hand to signal dog.

After a few repetitions, get the treat out of your hand. Be sure to continue to keep your hand flat. Don't forget: Dogs watch our body language, and a curled hand looks different from a flat hand.

After a few days, you should be able to give the hand signal and say the word "Stand" before the behavior. As with the "Sit" and "Down," don't repeat it a second time. You can just hold your position and wait for the dog to think. If after 10 full seconds he doesn't "Stand," just start over with the earlier steps for a day or two.

You can start to add petting into the "Stand" in preparation for handling and grooming. Begin with a gentle touch, and gradually add real petting.

Miss Manners Would Be Proud: Door Etiquette

Let's say your dog won't sit quietly at the door and charges through each time you open it. You let him do this. Winter comes, your stoop is a sheet of ice, your dog pulls you through the door, and you fall down and hurt your back. Should you be angry at your dog? Nope! *You* trained your dog to charge through the door in the first place!

So what should you do? The obvious solution is to teach a "wait at the door until I release you to go through," or "proper door etiquette." Follow these steps for the house and the car doors:

1. Approach a door with the dog.

2. Ask the dog to "Sit" or "Down." (Be sure to train this before working in the door context.)

3. Put your hand on the doorknob.

4. If the dog stays in position, reinforce the dog.

5. If he moves, ask him to "Sit" again and don't take your hand off of the doorknob.

6. Repeat until the dog stays in position.

7. Then turn the knob without opening the door.

8. If the dog stays in position, reinforce the dog. If he moves, ask him to "Sit" again and don't take your hand off of the doorknob.

9. Repeat until the dog stays in position.

10. Now it's time to actually open the door a tiny bit. If he moves, ask him to "Sit," or you can say "Sit" while you open the door. Reinforce the dog if he doesn't move.

Continue in this manner, opening the door more and more while continuing to reinforce the "Sit" and "Stay" behavior.

When you can successfully go through the door you're halfway there! Now it is time to reinforce the dog for looking back to you once you're both through the doorway. This will come in handy when there are distractions on the other side of the door. Do it this way:

1. Once through the door, say your dog's name.

2. When he looks back, ask for a "Sit" and reinforce him for looking back.

3. Repeat until the dog automatically looks back to you when going through a door without a verbal reminder from you.

(Photos by P. Dennison)

Proper door etiquette coming out of the house and car door.

(Photos by P. Dennison)

The dog should learn to automatically look back at you after going through doors.

I'm Not Dead—My Tail Is Still Wagging: "Settle" and "Rollover"

"Settle" means to have the dog lie down on his side and stay there. You may also call it "Dead Dog," "Rest," or "Flat." Rollover is obvious—the dog rolls over. Both of these behaviors are useful in handling, grooming, and vet visits.

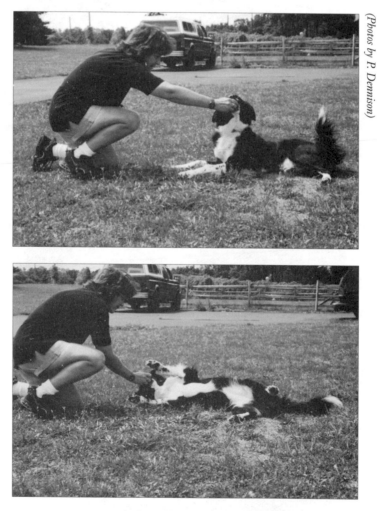

(Photos by P. Dennison)

Luring the dog into a "Settle."

(Photo by P. Dennison)

Luring the dog from a "Settle" into a "Rollover."

"Settle"

"Settle" is a great behavior for the dog to learn. The uses are many: veterinarian visits, calm behaviors, tick and flea patrol, or any type of physical exam you may need to do. Here's how to teach your dog:

1. Have the dog in a "Down."

2. Place your hand with a treat in front of the dog's nose.

3. Lure his head around slowly so that his nose is now facing his rear end.

4. When his elbow collapses under him, move the treat slowly around so that his head is flat on the ground. Click and treat.

5. If the dog gets up, don't worry; just try again.

Right now your hand cue is a big circle, but you can quickly change it to just be a small circle with your hand or finger. To get the "Stay" part of this exercise, use your pointer finger touching the ground as a helper cue, and then feed the treats from that hand. Fade out the treats in that hand as quickly as possible. It usually takes only a few days.

Once the dog is comfortable with the "Settle," you can add in gentle petting or an exam of genital areas and feet, always clicking and treating the dog for not moving. If the dog moves away, just try again—perhaps you went too fast or were petting in a place he's uncomfortable with.

(Photo by P. Dennison)

Adding the examination during the "Settle."

You can also be very creative when adding a cue word for this and other trick behaviors. Think about it ahead of time so that you can add in the cue word or hand motion from the beginning. My absolute favorite line is, "I am going to hypnotize you. When I count to three and snap my fingers, you will fall asleep. One, two, three (snap)." The snapping of your fingers is the cue for the dog to "Settle."

"Rollover"

"Rollover" is the obvious next step after teaching the "Settle." "Rollover" is a great behavior to teach because it gets the dog acclimated to someone leaning over him. Here's what to do:

1. Once your dog is in the "Down" position, use the same luring movement that you started with doing the "Settle."

2. Now, instead of luring your dog's head to lay flat on the ground, continue to lure so that he rolls over completely. This may mean (depending on the size of dog you have) that you'll have to lean over him.

3. As soon as he rolls over, click and treat.

If he doesn't roll over right away or is nervous about you leaning over him, be sure to break down the steps into smaller ones. At each step of his head moving in the correct direction, click and treat. Be sure to move your hand slowly and try not to get too excited about him "getting it" instantly. Small steps in easy training sessions will keep him interested in the game.

The Least You Need to Know

- "Sits," "Downs," and "Stands" are more important than you think.

- Training proper door etiquette can save both you and your dog some injuries.

- Hands off training will get you there faster.

- Settling and rolling over come in handy in many situations.

Chapter 13

Loose-Leash Walking

In This Chapter

- 🏠 Why do dogs pull? To get to the other side!
- 🏠 The relationship thing, again
- 🏠 Leash-walking exercises and games
- 🏠 Use sniffing to your advantage

This is such an important topic, and one most people can relate to, that this chapter is devoted entirely to loose-leash walking. I've known some fantastic dogs that have been dumped in shelters, just because they pull on the leash. There are many nuances to walking on a loose leash and this is not just a simple behavior.

But I Love Choking Myself: Why Dogs Pull

You want to peacefully walk your dog, but your dog all of a sudden picks up a scent and takes off at warp speed. Your walks have become a nightmare and you almost wish you could untrain his housetraining because cleaning up messes on the carpet would be easier than walking him.

(Photo by P. Dennison)

A dog taking his owner for a walk.

You sweat, you yank back, in desperation you use a choke or prong collar, you curse and scream. Finally, you declare your dog is stupid, stubborn, willful, disobedient, or even dominant. What has actually happened is that you've systematically trained your dog to pull on the leash. Congratulations! You did it! You learned how to activate his opposition reflex, and you taught him that to get where he wants to go, he has to pull you down the street.

Dogs do not pull to drive you insane, nor do they pull "because they can," and they truly haven't been up all night, scheming in their devious doggie minds how to annoy you to death by giving you whiplash. Really.

However there are very specific reasons why dogs pull on the leash and do a great imitation of dislocating your shoulder.

Because We Follow

The number one reason why dogs pull in leash: Because we follow. Behavior is reward driven. If choking himself gets him what he wants—to move forward in any direction he so chooses—then guess what? He'll continue to pull.

Pulling on the leash then becomes a learned behavior, and a very strong one at that. "Fanatical" and "overzealous" are words that can used to describe many dogs' leash-wrenching techniques, as they perfect their performance.

Of course, they want to make us happy. "You like it when I pull a little, so you should like it even better when I pull a lot." So what starts out as a little pulling can quickly become a "run for your money, might as well wear roller blades" event because "more is better," right?

To Get to the Other Side

The number two reason why dogs pull on the leash: to get to the other side. There are actually two parts to this. Number one, the outside world is an exciting and wonderfully smelly place for a dog. It is a veritable smorgasbord of scent. And number two, the dog forgets we exist.

Scent is extremely important to a dog—after all, they're predators—yes, even a Maltese or Miniature Poodle. Dogs process a great deal of information about their world through their noses. We've all seen our dogs sniff one single blade of grass for 15 minutes and think this is a bit excessive. However, it's not without meaning for a dog. He finds out who was here and when, who is in season, and how many bitches and how many males have been there.

 Doggie Data

Did you know that a dog has 20 to 40 times more olfactory receptors than a human? Some dogs can find bodies, dead or alive, by following scents of shed skin flakes, sweat droplets, and scent mists for as a long as 105 hours and as far as 135 miles. Many dogs can also "fore smell" seizures in humans and detect skin-cancer cells.

170 **Part 3:** Let the Games Begin! Positive Training in Action

Part two of "getting to the other side": The dog has completely forgotten that we exist and we are no more important than a speck of dust. There are many reasons for this seeming lack of respect. Most people train their dogs in the living room and never "take it on the road." They're then shocked and dismayed that their dog "blows them off" once outside.

Canine Caveats _____

A dog can be easily taught to "blow you off." This is effort-lessly accomplished by continually calling his name eight zillion times when he's obviously engaged in some sort of hunting behav-ior and has no intention of responding to you at that time. Your dog really isn't blowing you off; he just has his own agenda at the moment. The solution is to build your relationship so that your agenda becomes your dog's agenda.

The biggest challenge we all come up against is to be more interesting and reinforcing to our dogs than spit on the sidewalk. Whether you're doing pet training or competition training, or whether you're a first-time dog owner or an accomplished dog trainer, becoming more fascinating than the environment continues to be a challenge.

That challenge can be drudgery or it can be fun, enlightening, and immensely rewarding if you have the right attitude. The key here is one of the basics of positive dog training: the relationship between you and your dog. There are many facets to building a bond with your dog. Associative learning—making sure fun things happen around you at all times—tops the chart. Also up there are having patience at all times, manners training, and being variable and unpredictable in when and how you reinforce your dog.

The Opposition Reflex

The number three reason why dogs pull on the leash: Because we activate their opposition reflex, which causes them to pull against anything that's pulling against them.

Try this test. Have someone stand next to you. Push on that person's arm. If that person doesn't want to fall, that person will push back so that he or she isn't knocked over. Now pull on the person's arm. If the person doesn't want to be yanked toward you, he or she will pull back.

Okay, now that you know why everything you've tried so far to stop your dog from pulling on the leash hasn't worked, let's get to what does work.

Doggie Data

All animals, including humans, have an opposition reflex. It's a natural action that we can't control. When the doctor taps your knee with that little hammer and your leg jerks, you have no control over that response. Think about it. One person bumps into another person. That person pushes back, perhaps harder. Tempers flare, and voila! Instant bar brawl.

Building an Outdoor Relationship

The first step to loose-leash walking is building your relationship outdoors. This isn't hard, but it does take some forethought. You have to teach your dog that there is "no such thing as a free lunch." After all, we have to work for a living, and the dogs should, too.

Attention, Please!

Before teaching any behavior outdoors, you must build your relationship and get the dog's attention. Follow these steps—hand-feed your dog most of his intake of food for behaviors rather than for "free" in his bowl and "his wish is your command":

1. Take your dog's daily ration of food, put it in your pockets or pouch, and go outside.

2. Work on eye contact, name recognition, "Sits" and "Downs," and anything else your dog may know how to do at the moment. (For more details, see Chapters 10 and 12.)

3. If your dog is too stimulated by your yard, just wait. Bring a book if you have to and just sit on the porch. Whenever he gives you some kind of attention, reward it.

Pooch Pointers

If the dog doesn't notice you exist, ask yourself questions such as "Are the distractions too much for my dog to handle at this time in his training?" "Did I go from the living room to the football game in one step?" "Was I distracted or not in the mood?" Always set the dog up to succeed and he will!

Canine Caveats

You must have this very simple foundation—getting and keeping your dog's attention—before moving onto the next step. Try loose-leash walking without it and you'll get tight leash pulling.

4. If, after about 10 minutes, he still hasn't noticed that you exist, put him back in the house and in his crate for a few minutes and try again later.

Continue to do this for a few days—feeding for attention and simple behaviors. Now move to a new location and start all over, waiting patiently for attention and simple behaviors. Every few days, move to a new location and repeat all of the preceding steps.

The dog has to know that you aren't a dead tree stump. After about one to two weeks of practicing in about five to seven spots, you'll be ready to start training for loose-leash walking.

Moving Backups

This is the first step to loose-leash walking/heeling. This also teaches the dog to pay attention to you while you're both moving. Dogs think about what they're looking at, so if they aren't looking at you, then guess what? They aren't thinking about you, either.

Follow these steps:

1. Get your dog's attention and take a few steps backwards. Click and treat if the dog follows you. You're not looking for eye contact yet—you just want him to follow you.

2. Don't lure your dog with cookies—have your hands down by your sides. If the dog mugs your hands, put them behind your back.

3. Take a few more steps back and click and treat every few steps.

4. Gradually increase the amount of steps you back up before clicking and treating. Now you can ask for eye contact.

Pooch Pointers

By "asking for eye contact," I don't mean that you should say your dog's name repeatedly or say "watch." Do this right and your dog will automatically look at you. Just wait for eye contact, click and treat, and then move back a few more steps.

(Photo by P. Dennison)

A dog and his handler doing moving backups.

174 Part 3: Let the Games Begin! Positive Training in Action

If your dog looks away you can either …

🏠 Continue to back up and click and treat when he comes back into position.

🏠 Stop moving and wait for the dog to reengage with you (by giving you eye contact); then continue to back up and then click and treat.

Don't You Like Looking at My Butt? Follow the Leader

My favorite way to teach loose-leash walking is to actually start without a leash. If your dog wants to stay with you without a leash, then adding the leash is a piece of cake. To start this, I like to play "follow the leader" on either a 50-foot long line or off leash completely in a safe, fenced-in area.

Doggie Data

When I switched over from traditional training to positive training, playing the long-line game was great practice for me to get rid of my old habit of popping and jerking my dog's leash. You can't pop and jerk if you aren't holding a leash. In addition, it really forced me to build my relationship, rather than rely on a leash to keep my dog with me.

Arm yourself with wads of yummy treats and follow these steps:

1. Give your dog one treat.

2. Walk away. (Don't use any verbal cues or commands with this game. You want your dog to stay with you because he *wants* to, not because you're forcing him to do so with the leash, or constantly prodding him verbally.)

3. If your dog follows you, feed him treats and pet and praise him for a full 20 seconds.

4. Now change direction. If your dog stays with you, reinforce him again for a full 20 seconds. After each reinforcer, change direction.

5. Repeat until your dog stays by your side as you move around.

6. If your dog comes toward you but charges on ahead, turn around and walk away from him. This is where you don't want to look at his butt. The name of this game is called "follow the leader," and he isn't the leader. You are.

7. Keep repeating until your dog stays with you.

Canine Caveats

Some dogs are successful with this game within a few minutes and some dogs take hours to stay around their owners. If your dog is one of the few that won't focus on you, please don't be angry. Just backtrack and work on more focus at home first.

Look Ma, No Hands: Loose-Leash Walking

Once your dog is successful in wanting to stay with you off leash, you can now add the leash. Above all, remember, the leash is *not* a tool. It is a safety net!

Try to start this in a low-distraction area. As always, you want to set the dog up for success as much as possible. After all, I bet you didn't learn to drive on a major highway—you probably started in an empty parking lot. Gradually work up to heavy distractions. The higher the distraction level, the higher value your reinforcers should be.

Because this is a slightly different context (the dog is now on a leash), you may want to go back to the basics:

Pooch Pointers

If you've taught your dog to pull on a collar, you may want to consider switching to a harness. My favorite type of harness is available from Black Ice, listed in Appendix B.

1. Start walking, encouraging the dog (verbally) to follow.

2. If the dog pulls, that's your cue to stop any forward movement.

3. If the dog relaxes his pulling or looks back to you, call the dog to you, take a few steps, and then reward the dog with a treat.

4. The dog may pull again, so get ready to stop. Repeat a billion times. (Actually, after about 10 minutes the dog usually starts to pull less.)

Canine Caveats

Once you start this exercise, you can't go back to letting the dog pull ever again! In the beginning stages of this game be sure to take your time—bring a book with you, get up earlier, do whatever you have to do to not rush the process.

5. Once the dog is pulling less, start rewarding if the dog *isn't* pulling! Even if the dog takes only one step of loose-leashing walking, reward him! Start with a few steps of loose-leash walking, and pretty soon you'll be able to walk a mile without dislocating your shoulder!

How to Turn Your Worst Distraction into Your Greatest Ally

I can hear you groaning already! Dogs, kids, leaves, planes, cars, bicycles, deer, squirrels, birds, smells of all kinds, cats—the list is endless and frustrating. How can you use these distractions to your benefit? Build a strong positive relationship with your dog and become your dog's benevolent "Higher Power."

You've laid the groundwork by hand-feeding your dog for behaviors for a few weeks and now you have his attention outside. You've been practicing "follow the leader," and some loose-leash walking in a relatively distraction-free area. You're doing a great job!

Pooch Pointers

After the first week, continue to hand-feed for behaviors two to three times per week and you'll keep your dog focused on you.

Once you've built a solid foundation, you can now use the distractions that have driven you crazy to help build your relationship to an even higher level.

Use his sniffing as a reward for walking nicely by your side. Follow these steps:

1. Get a few steps of loose-leash walking (perhaps starting on a parking lot—let's make it easy for the dog to succeed).

2. Then run over to some grass and while you point to the ground, say "Go Sniff."

3. Let him have a penny's worth of sniffing and then verbally encourage him, without using the leash to drag him (or lure him with food or toys if you have to the first few times), to come back to you.

4. Heavily reward his recall, even if at first it wasn't all that prompt.

5. Do a few more steps of loose-leash walking and reward again with some sniffing.

Within a few repetitions, you should see your dog start to sniff less and less and be interested in you for longer periods of time. Why should this be so? Because you've ceased to be a barrier to his fun and are now his active partner.

The Least You Need to Know

- Dogs pull because we follow, because they want to smell things, and because of the opposition reflex.

- Build your outdoor relationship first before teaching loose-leash walking.

- Never let the dog pull again once you've decided to teach loose-leash walking.

- Stop being a barrier to your dog's fun; use what he wants as a reward for walking nicely.

Chapter 14

Stop in the Name of Love: Teaching the Stays

In This Chapter

- 🏠 Learning to stay the way whales do
- 🏠 The three "Ds": distance, duration, and distractions
- 🏠 Wait right there!
- 🏠 Teach your dog that patience will be rewarded

The "Stays" are almost as hard to teach as loose leash walking. We spend much of our time training the dog to stay close to us and heavily reward them for it. Now we want them to stay way over there. Can't we humans make up our minds?

"Stays" are difficult to teach but very important, and can be life-saving for our dogs. They are helpful when you have a multiple dog household to stop them from getting in your way and tripping you while you are running for the phone.

"Stays" are useful for the vet's office, grooming, toenail clipping, or waiting at the front door, car door, and crate door before you release them. They're essential for competition obedience, agility, sheep herding, and any other dog sport.

In addition, "Stays" are great for teaching your dog to "stay on his mat," so that you can eat dinner without being mauled or without the dog begging (although all begging behavior is caused by someone feeding the dog from the table, thus reinforcing the dog for begging).

Take a Load Off: "Sit," "Down," and "Stand Stay"

Obviously, to start teaching the "Stays," you must already have trained "Sit," "Down," and "Stand" behaviors. Please review Chapter 12 before attempting "Stays."

There are many positive methods for teaching "Stays." However, I've found one method to be the most effective. It was developed by the trainers at SeaWorld, and this is how they teach "Stay" to the myriad animals they work with. I call it the "Shamu Stays" method. It works extremely well for "Sit," "Down," and "Stand." Heck, if it's good enough for killer whales, sea lions, sea otters, and dolphins, it's good enough for Fido!

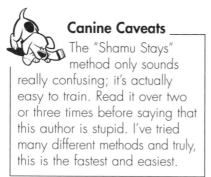

Canine Caveats

The "Shamu Stays" method only sounds really confusing; it's actually easy to train. Read it over two or three times before saying that this author is stupid. I've tried many different methods and truly, this is the fastest and easiest.

Before you start, make copies of the blank charts in Appendix C and use them "on the road."

Finding Your Dog's Threshold

To start teaching "Stays," you must know your dog's threshold—how long he'll stay in one position without moving and without any other cues from you. To figure it out, follow these steps:

1. Ask your dog to "Sit" or "Down." (Don't say "Stay.")

2. Step right in front of him.

3. Start the timer.

4. Stand there passively.

5. Stop the timer the instant your dog gets up. Don't say anything when he breaks the "Sit" or "Down."

Pooch Pointers

If you ask your dog to "Sit" and he sits and then goes into a "Down," this does not constitute a "Stay." "Stay" means "stay in that position until I come back and release you."

Repeat this three times (not necessarily in the same session). Take the lowest time (for example, four seconds) and that's your dog's threshold, which is where you will start.

Training the "Stays"

Take the dog's threshold time and subtract one second. (Using our previous example, now you have three seconds.) That's the time at which you'll *remind* the dog to "Stay." The reason you subtract one second is that's one second *before* the dog broke the "Stay." Then multiply three seconds by two, which equals six seconds ($3 \times 2 = 6$). At six seconds, you click and treat (C/T). Then you release to start a new trial. Do this so the dog is successful three times in a row (not in the same training session) and then move on to the next level.

In the beginning, do your "Stays" with the dog right in front of you. Build up length of time first, then you can build up your distance away from the dog. The following is a sample worksheet you can use to keep track of the levels. See Appendix C for blank versions you can use yourself.

Sample Stay-Training Sheet

Level One

Say "Down." Remind ("Down") at **3** seconds.

C/T (click and treat) and release at **6** seconds.

Repeat three times, move on to the next time level.

Level Two

Say "Down." Remind ("Down") at **5** seconds.

C/T and release at **10** seconds.

Repeat three times, move on to the next time level.

Level Three

Say "Down." Remind ("Down") at **9** seconds.

C/T and release at **18** seconds.

Repeat three times, move on to the next time level.

Level Four

Say "Down." Remind ("Down") at **17** seconds.

C/T and release at **34** seconds.

Repeat three times, move on to the next time level.

Level Five

Say "Down." Remind ("Down) at **33** seconds.

C/T and release at **1 minute, 6** seconds.

Repeat three times, move on to the next time level.

Level Six

Say "Down." Remind ("Down") at **1 minute, 5** seconds.

C/T and release at **2 minutes, 10** seconds.

Repeat three times, move on to the next time level.

Continue until you reach the desired time level.

Can you see the pattern? Even if you aren't good in math, this should be easy for you. You can see how simple it is to go from a three-second stay and build up to two minutes and ten seconds in six steps. Just continue for however long you want to teach your dog to "Stay." When you get three tries *in a row* correct, move up to the next level. If you get three in a row that are not correct, move down a few seconds and start again.

Watch for distraction levels as well. Start this with no or low distractions and gradually increase the distractions once you build up to the time level you want and need.

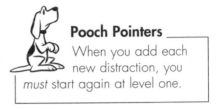

Pooch Pointers
When you add each new distraction, you *must* start again at level one.

If your dog breaks at any point, you must ignore him for about 15 seconds and then just reset the session. Make sure the dog won't run out in traffic when you ignore him. Be prudent. Be safe.

During the beginning stages of this training, it helps to have someone holding the timer for you, telling you when to remind and when to click and treat. Once you've built up to more than 18 seconds, it's easier for you to do it by yourself.

The Outer Limits: Adding Distance

Once you've built up to your optimum time using "Shamu Stays," it's now time to add distance. Don't go from standing right in front of your dog to expecting him to stay when you move 20 feet away. Start by moving only a foot away at first and start back at level one. You'll very quickly be able to move on to the next levels because your dog now has an idea of how this works.

Pooch Pointers
Be sure you turn your back on your dog as you walk away. Too many people back away from the dog, repeating the mantra "Stay, Stay, Stay." Then when they finally turn away from the dog, the dog breaks position and they wonder why.

The next step is to move two feet away from your dog, again, going back to level one. From there, you go three feet, then four, then five, and so on until you've gained the distance you want.

This method may seem very time consuming and too complicated, but it really is quite simple once you get the hang of it, and it's very effective.

Do It Anyway: Adding Distractions

Next up—the dreaded distractions! The list is endless. Kids, bikes, cars, dogs, people, birds, squirrels, and deer—you name it, it can be a distraction.

Start out with mild distractions—say one other person walking slowly around. Then have the person walk faster, then jog, then run. Then add another person, and another. You can start to add toys (not teasing the dog) and other types of distractions. Always be sure you add them slowly and always set the dog up for success.

Pooch Pointers

If you've done your homework, building your relationship and recalls amidst distractions, this shouldn't be too hard.

Be sure that once you start a higher intensity of distractions you go back to level one of the time chart. If the dog breaks, say to yourself, "No big deal," and just try again. Please stay away from any verbal "corrections." Silence works best.

Wait a Minute!

Many people use just one word—"*Stay*"—to mean a few different things. I like using two words: "*Stay*" and "*Wait.*" To me, they have different meanings. "Stay" means, "you stay there until I come back to you." "Wait" means, "wait there until I give you another cue." If you feel more comfortable using just one word, that's not a problem as long as you're clear in your direction. Do what you'll remember and what you'll be consistent with.

Two important uses of the "Stay"/"Wait" are to have the dog go to his mat and "Stay" there, and to "Wait" for dinner.

Go to Your Mat

Let's teach your dog to go to his mat. You may not think this is any big deal and that your dog doesn't need to know this, but it can be a very useful behavior.

If your dog is bugging you and you're busy, you can tell him to go to his "Mat," "Bed," or "Place"—whatever word you want to use. For dogs that have been reinforced for begging at the table, this is great to use. Basically, this is "target training." You're teaching your dog to "target" the mat and lie down on it and stay there. Follow these steps:

1. Have a mat or bed set up.

2. Sit in a chair about five feet away.

3. Throw cookies onto the mat and don't say anything yet.

4. As the dog steps on the mat, click and throw some more treats.

5. Repeat this about 24 times.

6. If the dog goes back to the mat of his own accord, click and throw treats. (We're now getting the behavior, then rewarding, rather than "luring" the dog onto the mat with the treats.)

At this point you still won't say anything to the dog. Get the full behavior, *then* give it a name. Dogs aren't really listening to us, anyway, and do better if we're quiet and let them think.

Now stop throwing cookies onto the mat. Look at your dog. Once he has also engaged your eye contact, look at the mat. Look at his face again and then look at the mat. If he looks at the mat or goes over to the mat, click and throw the treat on the mat. If he doesn't move, look at him again and then stare at the mat. For any movement toward the mat, be it head or body movement, you should click and throw cookies onto the mat.

Take the tape off of your mouth now—you can start talking! Follow these steps:

1. Once your dog goes to the mat either on his own or with the help of your eye, as he steps on the mat, say "go to your mat/place/bed" (whatever you want to call it).

2. Then click and treat the behavior.

3. Repeat this about 10 times.

4. Then do a test. When he's off the mat, say, "Go to your mat" and wait—see what he does.

5. If he goes to the mat, click and jackpot. If he doesn't, just backtrack.

6. Once your dog goes to the mat on a regular basis, go to him (because you're at least five feet away) and lure him into a "Sit" and then a "Down" and reward the "Down." I ask you to go to him because if you're any real distance from him, he'll get off of the mat and come to you to "Sit" and "Down." So, you need to teach him to work away from you for this exercise, which is why you have to either lean forward or move forward to help him in the beginning.

Very quickly, your dog will, upon hearing you say, "Go to your mat," go to the mat and lie down. Now, you have to build distance, duration, and changing *location*.

Doggie Data

My dog Cody taught me (without speaking one word of English) that by staring in the direction I want a dog to look, he'll turn his head that way. After I gave each of my dogs a bone, Cody came up to me after about 10 minutes, whining and turning his head repeatedly. I normally ignore him when he whines because I don't want to reinforce whining. However, I did glance at him out of the corner of my eye and realized he was looking at Beau and then back to me. Beau had stolen Cody's bone and he wanted me to get it back for him. Try it sometime—it is just too cool! And you never know, you may just find a use for it someday.

Changing location is great to work on—move the mat to different parts of the house and yard. Wouldn't it be great to go to a softball game, bring your mat, and ask the dog to go to his mat and he does it! *And* stays there! And doesn't annoy the other people there! Wow!

You'll also need to build distance. Let's say you're in the kitchen and the mat is in the living room. Your dog wants attention, but you're talking on the phone and cooking dinner and you're transferring hot things from the stove to the table—not a good time for your dog to decide "It's *playtime!!*" That's a perfect time to tell your dog to go to his mat.

When building distance, be sure to move away from the mat only a few feet at a time. Just as when you were teaching "Stays," building distance slowly is important to the success of the behavior.

Wait for Dinner

Waiting for dinner may not seem like a behavior you'll need, but it's an excellent and simple way to introduce the word *"Wait"* into your dog's vocabulary. I like it because it teaches self-control to the dog so that he doesn't get pushy and forceful around food.

Follow these steps:

1. Put a few pieces of food in a bowl on the counter.

2. Ask the dog to "Sit."

3. Start to put the bowl on the floor.

4. If at any time he moves out of position, take the bowl away.

5. Remind the dog to "Sit" again.

> **Canine Caveats**
> Pushiness around food or toys is not acceptable behavior. Many people misinterpret this behavior as being dominant, when in fact, this is just the behavior of an untrained, spoiled dog who was probably reinforced in the past for being obnoxious.

6. Repeat steps three and four. Don't add the word *"Wait"* yet—again, silence is best. Get the behavior first—then name it. After a few repetitions of steps three and four, you won't even have to remind the dog to "Sit" again—he will most likely fix himself.

7. Once the dog waits for even one second, click and release him to the food bowl.

8. As soon as he waits for two seconds, you can say the word *"Wait."*

9. You can increase the "Wait" time to be as long as you wish.

This easily transfers to "Wait" in the car, in the crate, or at the door, all of which may just save his life one day. "Stays" can be boring to teach, but the benefits are enormous, so please don't skimp on training them.

The Least You Need to Know

🏠 "Shamu Stays" is the best method of teaching "Sits," "Downs," and "Stays."

🏠 Start out building duration with little or no distraction; then add in distance to your "Stays."

🏠 Once you have distance and duration, you can add in distractions.

🏠 Practice "Go to your mat" and "Wait for the food bowl" to build your dog's patience and self-control.

What to Do If Your Dog Makes a Mistake

In This Chapter

- If at first you don't succeed, proceed!
- Finally, a *real* reason to clean your house!
- Don't get mad …
- Necessity is the mother of invention

If a dog makes a mistake, you need to stop and look at the situation. Did you make the mistake—giving wrong or different cues or pushing the dog beyond his limits? Did you train the dog in enough contexts with enough correct repetitions? Please stop blaming the dog. If you teach a behavior incorrectly or don't train enough, then it isn't the dog's fault if he responds incorrectly.

Let's look at some different positive options to pursue when your dog makes a mistake. Not everything works for every dog or each situation, but there's always a positive solution if you take the time to look for it.

Give Me a "P": Proceed, Put It on Cue

Two easy strategies for dealing with an incorrect response are to proceed and to put it on cue. These methods are great because they give you the chance to regroup, rethink, and go scream in the closet if you're getting angry. They also give you the opportunity to be creative in stopping some behaviors that are less than wonderful.

Proceed: Move On to Something Else

After three tries, if your dog just isn't "getting it" today, instead of repeating the routine again and again (which can be seen as a punishment because the dog is not being reinforced for the "mistakes"), move on to something else or give both of you a breather.

This also gives *you* the opportunity to rethink your training strategy. It's very important to know exactly how to teach each behavior before you even take the dog out for training. Trainers at SeaWorld and most of the positive dog trainers I know do this. They all get together and discuss in detail what each session will entail:

- What behavior they will work on
- What approximation of that behavior they will accept
- How many repetitions they will do
- What they will do if the animal doesn't respond correctly
- What the reinforcers will be
- How many minutes each session will last
- How many minutes of downtime between each session there will be
- How many total sessions to have per day

Put It on Cue

This means to cue and reinforce the "bad" behavior you don't like so that the dog learns to perform the "bad" behavior only on cue. Then don't ever give the cue!

I did this with Beau, one of my Border Collies. On rainy days I have towels by the back door to wipe the dogs' feet as they come in from the backyard mud field. Well, Beau thought that was really cool and would steal the towels and start to shred them.

So, I put the "towel stealing" behavior on cue. I call it "mop the floor" (because he likes to shake the towel, pretending that he's killing it). In the beginning, I would say "mop the floor" for stealing a towel and then click and treat him. I did this dozens of times, and now on rainy days he will not take a towel unless I say "mop the floor."

As they say, "if you can't beat 'em, join 'em." Or in the dog-training world we say "put it under *stimulus control* and never give the cue!"

 Muttley Meanings
Stimulus control means the dog responds promptly to a cue in any and all situations. Some people say barking can be put under stimulus control, but I've never seen it work. Barking seems to be an incredibly self-reinforcing behavior for some dogs, and they'll do it anyway, cued or not.

Give Me an "A": Administration, Aid, Antecedent

Setting the dog up to be right is key here. It's counterproductive, not to mention silly, to set the dog up to fail and then get angry at him for failing.

Being frustrated is normal, and taking it out on the dog is easy. Your dog doesn't speak English and sometimes that makes training hard. However, there are easy answers.

Administration or Management

If your dog eats your shoes, put them away! If your dog gets into the garbage can, find one with a locking lid. If you know a certain stimulus upsets or overexcites your dog, use better judgment in introducing the stimulus to your dog. Then work on desensitizing your dog to it.

> **Doggie Data**
> You would be surprised at how many people actually believe their dogs are human and are born knowing household "rules." Dogs don't perform "bad" behaviors for spite, out of guilt, to get back at you, or for any other reason you may think up. Dogs do these things because you've either set them up to fail or because you've reinforced the dog for doing them.

Don't wait for something "bad" to happen—stop the behavior before it starts. Practicing "bad" behaviors does no one any good. Plus, it might make you angry and you may do something that you'll regret in the morning. After all, you would baby-proof a house, and you should doggie-proof it as well.

Aid

Give the dog an easier version of the behavior you're working on that he can solve successfully: shorten the time, distance, duration, or complexity.

For instance, let's say you're teaching your dog to "Stay," and you've built up to one minute in an area that has no distractions. Good job! Now you go to the ballgame, which is much more diverting than your empty living room. Don't ask your dog to "Stay" for one minute—he won't be successful. Try for three seconds to start and build slowly back up to one minute.

Antecedent

Give the dog some clear, intermediate helper cues so that he can understand more clearly what it is you want. This can be a verbal reminder cue, "Stay," or an additional hand signal. The key is not to do rapid-fire reminder cues—then you get stuck in the rut of "Sit-Sit-Sit-Sit-Sit" and sound like a machine gun. Dogs don't speak English, but they sure can count! Don't confuse them even more when your task is to help them.

In addition, be sure that your cues are consistent and accurate. If sometimes you call your dog to "Come" and you're standing up straight, and sometimes bending over, or sitting, or kneeling, you'll have one very confused doggie. If your cue for "Down" is normally a raised hand like a traffic cop but one day you just raise your hand high in the sky, don't be surprised when the dog looks at you blankly.

> **Doggie Data**
>
> Just for the heck of it, I decided to train my dog Shadow to move to the right, left, and back away from me, using my eyes only (with no head turns) as a cue. That's how small our signals can be and how extremely sensitive dogs are to our body language.

Give Me an "I": Incompatible, Ignore, Innovation

Now is the time to get a bit inventive. I've given you some of my favorite options to jump-start your creative juices. Incompatible behaviors will save your sanity, so teach your dog to do all of the behaviors in this book—they are all "incompatible" with fear, aggression, and nervousness. They also give the dog a "job" to do. If you don't give your dog a job, he will become self-employed, and you most likely won't like the career change.

Incompatible

Give your dog a command (one that he knows well) that's incompatible with the "bad" behavior he's doing at the moment. For instance, if you tell the dog to "Sit," that's an incompatible behavior to jumping.

He can't be jumping if he's sitting. Or, once your dog has excellent name recognition (see Chapter 12), you can say his name to get his attention and then give him a cue to a different behavior to keep him otherwise occupied.

Training incompatible behaviors is one of my favorite ways of solving behavior problems. Sometimes it just takes a bit of thought to come up with a solution.

If your dog goes crazy every time the doorbell rings, train him that the sound of the doorbell means, "Go to your crate." Let's say that every time your dog sees someone, he wants to fling himself at that person. Teach him that a person approaching is a cue to sit. Or if you want to allow him to approach a person, teach him to "Go Visit," meaning to go to the person you're pointing to and lie down—which is incompatible to jumping.

Ignore the Dog

If the dog is doing something bad, ignore him until he gives you a "good" behavior that you can then reinforce. For example, if your dog is barking at someone or something, just stand still until he's quiet, wait for 10 seconds, and then reinforce the quiet behavior. By yelling or petting to calm him down, you're actually reinforcing the inappropriate behavior, which is something I don't really think you want to do. If, after 15 seconds or so the dog hasn't regained control of himself, move away, redirect onto appropriate behaviors, and then reinforce the dog for "good" behaviors.

Canine Caveats

Please use good judgment when walking away from your dog during training. Don't disappear if the area isn't safe and secure to leave your dog.

If the dog is ignoring you, leave the area and have the dog search for you. Let him know that you aren't irrelevant or just a piece of furniture that happens to be at the end of the leash.

Doggie Data

Here's a quiz: Kate had problems with her 14-month-old dog, Chloe. Chloe was constantly jumping and biting for attention, and she'd been doing this since she was 12 weeks old. If she didn't get instant attention, Chloe would become more frantic and bite harder, especially if there was food around.

Question: Why was Chloe doing this and what can be done to stop it?

Answer: Kate admitted to reinforcing the jumping and mouthing by giving Chloe attention by petting or yelling at her. To fix Chloe's behavior, Kate should ignore inappropriate behaviors and reward her heavily for not bothering humans and for being calm around food; she could also teach Chloe to do really fast sits (sitting is incompatible with jumping and biting).

Innovation

Try changing your rewards to something new that the dog really craves. No matter how much you like M&M's, there's probably a level at which you will satiate, and the same thing happens to your dog. Use all different types of food, toys, silly games, petting, and praise to reinforce your dog.

Being variable and unpredictable is the key to enriching your dog's life and training. Chapter 9 has a full discussion on the "how" of variable reinforcement.

Give Me an "R": Repeat, Redirect, Recreation, Restrain

Watch and listen to your dog. If you pay attention to what your dog is telling you, most of the time you can come up with an easy solution. If you have a good relationship with your dog, he really does want to do what you're asking him. If all of a sudden he looks at you blankly, please don't assume he's stupid.

Repeat the Cue a Second Time

Try one more time by using clearer cues, such as a hand signal. Wait for at least 10 seconds before repeating the command so that the dog learns to perform immediately after the first command. Don't repeat the command a third time! You don't want your command to be "Sitsitsit!"

By waiting patiently for at least 10 seconds, you're giving the dog the opportunity to *think!* Remember when you were first learning a foreign language? Did you remember all of those new words the first time out? In addition, please don't forget—humans are a verbal species and dogs are not!

Redirect

Redirect to better behavior. If your dog eats the sofa, learn what he usually does just before eating the sofa—sniffing the floor, running around, barking, or whining—and stop the sofa destruction *before* it happens.

You can distract him with a toy when he just starts to think about eating the sofa, but be sure you don't then try to play with him *after* he has already started. This will only reinforce the sofa-eating behavior. You can still distract, but then give him at least three other behaviors to do and then reinforce him. Either put the dog in the crate or engage him in some stimulating activity.

Dogs that incessantly bark or chew are usually understimulated or bored or have been inadvertently reinforced (with your attention or bad timing of reinforcement) for doing the very behavior that's driving you crazy. Remember—behavior is reward driven!

Be sure to pay plenty of attention to your dog when he's not doing anything "bad!"

> **Canine Caveats**
>
> It's imperative to redirect before the behavior starts; otherwise, the dog learns, "Eat the sofa and my humans play with me. Wahoo!"

Recreation

Use tiredness to your advantage: A dog that is fully exercised, both mentally and physically, is less likely to bark, chew, jump up, or otherwise drive you insane.

Giving the dog enough vigorous exercise *with you* is excellent preventive therapy! My motto is: "A tired dog is a good dog." A placid walk around the block is not enough aerobic exercise to physically tire out most dogs. Playing fetch, swimming, playing with another dog, jogging, and hiking are all good ways to keep your dog fit and tire him out. This is the ultimate incompatible behavior: a sleeping dog can do no harm.

 Doggie Data

I prefer activities that the two of you can do together. Because associative learning (remember Ivan Pavlov?) is always happening, you might as well take advantage of it and pair yourself with all sorts of fun things for your dog. That way, you have a tired dog and a dog that associates good stuff with you. It's a win-win situation.

Restrain

Confine or contain the dog. But be sensible! If imminent danger threatens, get your dog out of there!

If the dog is veering off into traffic, or a loose dog bent on rearranging you or your dog's face is in attack mode, get out of there. Although it's preferable to wait out a "bad" reaction from your dog so that you can then reinforce "good" behavior, there are times when a fast retreat is best. If the dog is so incredibly overaroused that he's foaming at the mouth, spit is flying everywhere, and his eyes are glazed, then oops! Get him out of there—now!

There's time enough later, when everyone is calm, to assess the situation dispassionately and carefully. If the situation was something out of your control—such as a loose dog with no owner in sight— you can read Chapter 7, on familiarizing yourself with calming signals. Many times you can use these to "disarm" a dog that is showing aggressive behaviors.

Doggie Data _____

Patty was out with her dog Mike when they came upon a loose dog running around, growling at every dog in his path. There was no way of restraining the loose dog, so Patty quickly and calmly asked Mike to lie down (a calming signal). She kept Mike's attention on her, rather than risk him reacting to the errant dog. The instant Mike laid down, the approaching dog slowed his pace, sniffed Mike in a halfhearted fashion, and then went about his doggie way.

Above all, think about what *you're* doing to encourage your dog to behave in a certain way. If your dog does something you don't like on a regular basis, watch *yourself* to see whether you're inadvertently reinforcing the dog for doing that very behavior!

For instance, if your dog repeatedly steals your clothes and then you chase after him in a merry game of keep-away, your dog thinks "What fun, Mommy! Thanks!" Do you yell at the dog? (Remember—negative attention is still attention.) Now he thinks "Wow, Mom is turning purple *and* chasing me all over the house! Thanks, Mom!" Before getting angry, think to yourself, "What is the *dog* finding reinforcing?

So, we have now have a P, an A, an I, and an R. What does that spell? *Pair!* You and your dog are a pair, a team, best friends, and a match made in heaven! So, let's give the *dog* a b-r-e-a-k!

The Least You Need to Know

- If your dog doesn't respond correctly after three tries, move on to something else.

- Stop "bad" behaviors before they start; be a helper and set your dog up for success.

- If your dog does something bad, redirect him to an incompatible behavior, such as lying down.

- Get your human emotions out of dog training—they don't belong there!

Part 4 The Reality Show: Dogs and Your Lifestyle

Think you don't have time to train your dog? In three, five-minute sessions per day, you, yes you, *can* have the dog of your dreams! In Part 4, you'll see how to introduce your dog to your kids, how to get a new dog situated into your family and home, and how to train your dog while holding down a full-time job. And in case you're having problems, here are some tips for curing your dog's lapses in behavior.

Chapter 16

Adding a Dog to Your Household

In This Chapter

- 🏠 Your dog's own domain: crate training
- 🏠 Potty training
- 🏠 Good things happen when he's around
- 🏠 Spit, spat—resource guarding and fights

Adding a dog to your family takes patience and strategic planning. It also takes a real commitment on your part to remain calm and positive and not to forget *your* training of doggie body language.

Adding a second (or third, or …) dog is *not* easy; and at times during the beginning stages, you may want to kick yourself in the head for doing it. However, most of us who have multiple-dog households do survive and actually continue to add more and more, even though we swear at the time, "we will *never* do it again!"

Crate Training

Teaching your dog to love his crate is one of the best things you can do for your new best friend. Your dog will have to be crated many times in his life—for grooming, vet visits, or if he ever gets lost and is picked up by animal control.

Pooch Pointers

You can do a few things to ensure your dog comes home safe and sound if he ever gets lost:

- **Microchips:** Most veterinarians can insert a small micro-chip in the shoulder blade area. Most veterinarians, rescue groups, and shelters have a scanner and can scan the dog to get your contact information.

- **Tattoos:** Goes on the inner thigh. Two registries keep information on tattooed dogs. Be aware however, that many rescue organizations will not look for a tattoo, and they are harder to see on long-haired dogs.

- **Photos:** Always have a current photo on hand in case you need to put up flyers.

- **Emergency info:** When you are traveling with the dog, keep information in the car or your wallet in case you have an accident. Include contact numbers of friends that will take the dog, name of veterinarian, any medical information needed, and any behavioral issues the dog may have.

Crate training is essential for younger dogs or rescue dogs to help them not to soil or eat the house. If you don't want your dog jumping in bed with you at 2 A.M. to get you to play, you'll need to put him in the crate. You can also crate your young pup when company comes until you can train him not to jump on company.

Doggie Data

Martha brought her German Shepherd Nemo to class. One of her complaints was that the dog was chewing up everything in the house. When I recommended crate training, she told me that her husband flatly refused to crate train the dog because, "he wants the dog to learn not to chew furniture."

He was under the incredible misconception that Nemo wouldn't chew if he viewed the house and all it's contents as his own. After all, when her husband came home and beat the dog for chewing, "it was obvious to the man that Nemo *knew* what he did wrong." Hello?!?

The Benefits of Crate Training

The benefits of crate training (to both you and the dog) are numerous:

- 🏠 Makes house training easier—be it house soiling or chewing.

- 🏠 Gives the dog a safe, secure place to "get away from it all."

- 🏠 Manages the dog when you are busy and can't pay attention to him. This includes when visitors come, when you are leaving for work, when you're cooking dinner and the dog wants to play, and so on.

- 🏠 Helps you manage a multiple-dog household.

- 🏠 Enables your dog to cope with vet and groomer visits, where he will be crated.

- 🏠 Makes traveling with your dog easier, safer, and less stressful for both of you.

Canine Caveats

Letting a dog run loose in the car doesn't cut it with me. At the very least, use a seatbelt. *Never* put the dog in the front seat! Airbags can kill small children and will certainly kill your dog. I prefer a crate when traveling with my dogs. In fact, the criteria when I picked out my van was that it had to be big enough for four crates.

Crate-Training Instructions

Break up crate training into several different sessions. Before you start the first session, have lots of treats on hand (my definition of "lots" is about three Baggies filled with pea-size treats). Keep the door open and follow these steps:

1. Throw a handful of treats into the crate.

2. Stand back (so as not to pressure the dog) and let him go into the crate on his own.

3. Once he is done eating the treats, throw in more.

 **Doggie Data** _____

If you do your research well, you can find a breeder that actually crate trains all of their puppies before they leave the nest.

 Doggie Data _____

When I was a groomer, two Huskies came in for grooming and were not crate trained. One of them was so frantic that she bent the metal bars on the crate door with her teeth and was throwing up bile and blood. Needless to say, I called the owner to come and get the dogs and did not groom them.

Pretty soon, the dog will just stay in the crate, waiting for you to throw in more treats. This usually takes about 10 to 15 minutes.

In the next session, throw in a few cookies to "review" and then wait for the dog to go into the crate on his own. Then throw in wads of cookies as a reward (as opposed to a bribe) for going into the crate. Then follow these steps:

1. Call him out of the crate and then _look_ at the crate (don't say anything yet).

2. Once he goes back into the crate, reward him again heavily.

3. Repeat the preceding two steps five or six times.

In your third session, follow these steps:

1. Go over to the crate and look at it (still don't say anything).

2. When he goes back into the crate, reward him heavily.

3. Repeat this four to five times.

4. Then, as he is going into the crate (not before—pair the word with the behavior), say "Crate" or "Place" or whatever you want your word to be for telling the dog to go to his crate.

5. Reward heavily when he goes into his crate.

6. Repeat about five times

In your fourth session, repeat steps two and four from the preceding list. Then try to say the word "Crate" (or whatever) *before* he goes in, to see if he understands. If he goes into the crate, give him a mega jackpot of treats! Repeat this four to five times and then end the session.

At the fifth session, you'll start closing the door while the dog is comfortable going into his crate. Close the door for about five seconds, while he is still eating the last jackpot you gave him. Before he is done eating, open the door. Let him come out of the crate. Repeat a few times.

In later sessions, start gradually—and I mean gradually (a few extra seconds at a time; use a timer to keep you on track)—keeping the door closed for longer periods of time. You can even sit next to the crate while dropping food into it.

You can also use a special toy he gets only in his crate. I like Kong toys stuffed with nut butter or other gushy foods to keep them occupied. Continue to build up the duration your dog can stay in the crate to at least a full minute before you start to leave the room.

Canine Caveats

You must keep this slow. If at any time the dog whines, you have gone on too long. If the dog whines or barks, you cannot let him out of the crate until he is quiet. If you let the dog out of the crate while he is whining, he will learn to whine in his crate—a mega no-no!

Once you have mastered this, in future sessions, you can start leaving the room. Follow these steps:

1. Start by doing this for 1 second. Leave the room and instantly come back.

2. Reward the dog for being quiet and open the crate door.

3. Then leave for 2 seconds, then 3, then 4, and so on, *always setting the dog up to not whine.* Keep him busy with a Kong or a nice meaty *raw* bone.

Canine Caveats

Never, never use the crate as punishment. If your dog is being "bad," put him in his crate, but do it gently and unemotionally and give him a treat anyway. Putting him away *after* he has been "bad" teaches the dog *nothing,* but it keeps you from killing him!

You can also feed the dog his dinner in the crate, which will speed along his acclimation to the crate. Repeat all of the preceding steps until you can leave your dog in his crate for hours at a time. This will not take as long as it looks. I crate trained one dog, whom the owner said couldn't be crate trained, in 45 minutes.

The Bathroom Is Outside

Above all, know that house training is a human issue, not a dog issue. We are the ones that want and need the dog to use the outside latrine. They don't care at all. It is imperative to give the dog a great deal of access to the outside. If a dog is left alone in the house for long periods of time, he will have no choice but to eliminate in the house.

Doggie Data

Humans have opposable thumbs that can open doors. Dogs do not. Ergo, dogs cannot open doors. So, you'll just have to get up and take the dog out!

Have patience with your dog. You wouldn't yell at your child for soiling his diaper, so don't yell at your dog. Yelling might make you feel better, but think what association you are creating: Squatting around you is dangerous. Forget about "catching him in the act." Just ignore it and move on with your life.

Know When to Go

So, what is your option? Be smarter than he is! Note how soon after eating, sleeping, napping, playing, and drinking he usually "goes." If, for example he messes five minutes after eating, take him outside three minutes after eating.

Learn your dog's signs that he has to go. He is not some little kid that can cram his fists into his crotch, bend his knees, and look desperate. Common signs of "I gotta go!" are circling, whining, frantic look on his face, bent tail, hunched butt area, enlarged anus, and sniffing. If you are playing with him when you see any of these signs, stop playing and take him out; otherwise, you are asking for a puddle.

You can also teach your dog to go to the door when he needs to eliminate. As you cross the threshold, say "outside." Do this for a few weeks. Then when you think he has to go, ask him "outside?" and he will probably go to the door.

Heavily reward the dog *outside* when he does his business and in the same spot he went. *Do not* reinforce him after you're back in the house unless you want him to mess the house. When you can't be watching him, put him in a crate (my recommendation), in an exercise pen, or an on easily cleanable floor. If he does mess on carpeting, be sure to clean it instantly and thoroughly. Otherwise, that spot will forever smell like the bathroom to him.

Pooch Pointers

You can train your dog to ring a small bell on a string attached to the doorknob when he needs to go outside. This is easily accomplished by ringing the bell as you cross the threshold to take the dog out. After a few repetitions, teach the dog to touch the bell with his nose and then take him out whenever he rings it.

If you can't seem to read your dog's signs, tether him to you with a six-foot leash. This will force you to pay closer attention to him and you'll be able to get him out faster, with fewer accidents.

False Alarms and Accidents

There may be times when you take your dog out and he won't do his business. Then he comes back into the house and messes at your feet. Please don't get angry with him. That is just counterproductive. The next time you take him out, wait longer until he goes. If it takes 10 minutes, it takes 10 minutes. Bring a book, call your mother, or practice the multiplication tables in your head, but *do not* bring that dog back into the house until he is empty.

If after 15 minutes he still hasn't gone, put him in his crate, wait for 10 minutes, and try again. Continue to do this until he goes outside. Reward him heavily when he finally does go where you want him to go.

If he does mess the house, grab the nearest newspaper, roll it up, and hit yourself over the head while chanting, "I forgot to watch my dog, I forgot to watch my dog." If your dog laughs, praise him.

We Have Landed! When a Second Dog Comes Home

The best way to introduce a new dog to an existing dog is to do it in a neutral place that neither dog feels is "his." Off leash is better, and you should add in scads of food to the mix. You can hand-feed each dog simultaneously and also dump tons of food on the ground. Be careful though, if your dog guards food; if he does, throw the food in opposite directions to avoid any arguments.

Why would you feed the dogs together? Have you forgotten Pavlov already? Add in positive associations for both dogs from the very beginning and you'll have a better chance for success.

*Feeding two dogs at the same time, keeping them equidistant
from each other and the handler. Feed so that the dogs' heads
are turned away from each other to avoid conflicts.*

If you see a squabble, you must *not* punish either of the dogs.
If you do, you're setting them up for a lifetime of hatred—think
Hatfields and McCoys. You already learned in Chapter 4 what will
happen if you punish, so please avoid this at all costs.

No, You Can't Have It!

Food and resource guarding are common problems in a multidog
household. The resources a dog can guard can be you, other family
members, toys, beds (yours and his), food bowls, crates, and even
furniture.

Positive Solutions to Resource Guarding

The positive solution is to do the following:

- 🏠 Reinforce the more *dominant* dog for ignoring the subordinate dog. You can click and treat the dominant dog for attention while the subordinate dog is being a pest. Or you can click and toss treats to the dominant dog while you give petting to the subordinate dog.

- 🏠 Reinforce the more dominant dog for allowing the subordinate dog to get attention.

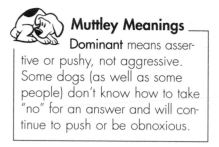

Muttley Meanings

Dominant means assertive or pushy, not aggressive. Some dogs (as well as some people) don't know how to take "no" for an answer and will continue to push or be obnoxious.

- 🏠 Reinforce any and all "pro-social" behaviors such as gentle tail wagging, playing, play bows, and mutual grooming.

- 🏠 Feed the subordinate dog first, so that the dominant dog learns a little patience.

If you reinforce the dominant dog for being dominant, then what will happen? He will become completely overbearing and out of control.

Doggie Data

Shadow is the pushiest dog in my pack of four. I used to feed him first because I was under the common misconception that "you should always feed the dominant dog first." That was a big mistake. I would feed him and then try to feed the other dogs. He would view *all* of the food as his. I had to constantly be on the lookout to stop potential fights.

As soon as I started feeding him last, all of the potential arguments stopped and he now waits patiently for his turn. Why should this be so? Because he now sees the other dogs being fed as a cue that his is coming up soon and he's actually much calmer when dinner time or "cookie time" rolls around.

Change, change, change everything! Switch blankets, crates, positions, food bowls—anything that your dog normally uses. It's imperative that you don't allow territory to be established and protected through your predictability. Reinforce any calming signals that you see because these are what stop squabbles from happening.

To avoid having one of your dogs become possessive of you, learn to position yourself into a triangle with you as the tip of it and the dogs as the base of it. Many dogs don't want to "share," but it's important that they learn to do it—for everyone's sake. This takes a bit of maneuvering on your part. Whenever I get a new dog, for at least a month, I make sure I can position myself so that no one is guarding me.

> **Pooch Pointers**
>
> You can also use this triangle position to teach dogs each other's names. Say "Rover," and then give Rover a treat. Then say "Fifi," and give Fifi a treat. Repeat a zillion times. This will come in handy when you want Rover to "Stay" there and Fifi to "Come." Just wait until you have three or four or more dogs! You'll be grateful that you taught them this.

Splitting Up

Dogs split other dogs to push them away, to guard things, or to avoid conflict from what they perceive as too rough play. You can use it effectively yourself, provided you're watching your dogs carefully. You must split at the earliest sign of conflict that you can see. It takes a great deal of practice to accomplish this and be successful, but it's well worth it in the long run.

When you split in between them, if they then move away from each other, be sure to reinforce both dogs for parting. This will help you to be successful in avoiding problems in the future.

> **Canine Caveats**
>
> When you split, be sure to go in from the back, never from the front. There's an important reason for this—there are no teeth in a dog's hind end.

(Photo by P. Dennison)

How to split the dogs if one gets pushy.

Make sure to crate train both dogs and use this to your benefit. Spend quality time with each dog alone and then when you do have both of them out together, make sure that good things always happen around the other dog. If you don't have the time to pay attention to both of them, then put them in their crates. This will give them some good "down time" to relax.

It's stressful even with the best mix of two personalities, so be sure to give both dogs some quiet time. On average, it usually takes about four to six months to have complete harmony in the house. Sometimes you may get lucky and it takes only a few days, but that's not the norm. Keep each of your sessions with both dogs short, positive, and successful.

If one dog is very pushy toward the other one, be sure to split and reinforce both dogs—the pushy one for going "over there and lying down," and the patient one for putting up with the pushy one.

It's very important for you to stay calm during all introductions and future training sessions. If you're stressed, what association do you think the two dogs will make? That's right—the dogs will get stressed because *you're* stressed. Even if they do have a "fight," it's vital that you remain calm.

Dangerous Squabbles?

Most squabbles are not serious. You may see teeth flashing and hear very scary noises, and you may think they're really killing each other. Don't be alarmed—be calm. Watch them carefully and you'll most likely see that no contact is made, and even if contact is made, most of the time they leave only spit and not punctures.

The most important things you can do are the following:

🏠 Remain calm.

🏠 Don't yell or hit or say *anything*.

🏠 Split between them if you can.

🏠 *Run* out of the room fast! The dogs will see you running away (dogs are attracted to movement) and will most likely follow you to see where you're going.

Most "arguments" last only a few seconds, although it seems that they go on forever. Yelling or hitting will incite them to aggress for longer periods of time and with more intensity. Silence is the way to go until all is calm. Then, if you want to, you can go in the bathroom, shut the door, and scream all you like. The next time, just be more cognizant of what they're doing, so that you can stop conflicts before they escalate.

Pooch Pointers

We humans have arguments all the time that mean nothing, and so do dogs. When we fight, we scream and yell, which is frightening to dogs because they're not humans and don't understand what we're saying. Their noises and their big white teeth are scary to us because we're not dogs and don't understand what they're saying, either.

What Am I Doing Wrong?

If you see that their squabbles are increasing in duration and intensity, put both dogs in their crates and sit down and think:

🏠 Have I been punishing them for arguments? Punishment includes yelling and hitting.

- Have I been giving them enough down time and alone time?

- Am I setting them up to fail by pushing them or forcing them to be pals?

- Am I watching them carefully, stopping conflicts before they start?

- Am I reinforcing all pro-social and friendly behaviors?

- Am I assuming that the original dog has to be "top dog" because he's been here longer, and forcing the new dog into a role of subordinate?

- Do the dogs view me as their own personal chew toy and are they guarding me, creating the fights?

Canine Caveats

When breaking up a dog fight, *never* grab them by the neck or collar—you're just asking to get bitten. If you're lucky enough to have another person with you, each of you should take hold of a dog's hind legs and tail simultaneously and move a large distance away so that you can contain the dogs. If you're by yourself, take control of the dog that seems to have the upper hand.

Be sure that you aren't the cause of their fights or contributing to the intensity. If you *really* feel you need to break them up physically, walk up slowly (if you run in screaming, the fight may take a turn for the worse) grab both dogs by the back legs and pull them apart as gently and calmly as you can. They will usually look back in surprise and then you'll be able to redirect them to a safer area.

Is Everybody Okay?

Once the dogs are separated and everyone is calm, check them over for any punctures. You can take care of most punctures yourself—just clean the wound, check it over the next day or two, and stop worrying. Even when dogs are playing, punctures can happen, so there's no need to freak out.

Continue to make sure that good things happen when they're together, ignore any squabbles, and heavily reinforce any pro-social, friendly behaviors, and your best friends will be buddies for life.

The Least You Need to Know

- Make sure all of your dogs are crate trained so that you can manage them better when you first bring the new dog home.

- Housetraining is an essential skill—but one that is driven by your needs and desires rather than your dog's.

- When you introduce a new dog to existing dogs, avoid any and all punishments, so that only positive associations are made between the two dogs. Watch them both carefully and reinforce all calm, playful behaviors.

- Most squabbles are harmless, but if they do escalate, look to yourself and your management of the two dogs.

Chapter 17

Kids and Dogs

In This Chapter

 Can you handle a kid and a dog together?

 Training the kids

 What will we do with Rover when the baby comes?

 To love, cherish, and honor (your dog)

Say you're watching television and you see this really cute commercial with a young child sitting on the ground, giggling, with a million puppies climbing all over him. The puppies are having fun and the kid is having fun. You look over to your spouse with tears of emotion in your eyes and say, "Honey, let's get Lily a puppy."

Think first, long and hard, and then think again. Then think one more time. Kids and dogs don't generally go well together. Puppies and dogs have sharp teeth and kids have delicate skin. Furthermore, moms are usually busy with kid activities and don't have time to properly train the puppy. This chapter explores all the issues involved when kids and dogs interact.

A Match Made in Heaven or ...?

If your child is very young, you'll need to manage the child and the dog both a great deal, making sure their needs are both met. As the puppy grows—and grow they do, much faster than we slow-developing primates—the adolescent dog may become too big and overwhelming for your still-tiny child.

If you have older children, as the puppy grows, the kids will take less and less interest in him—forget that they said, "I *promise*, I'll take the dog out, feed him his dinner, clean up his messes. I'll do everything! Please, pretty please!!"

You and I both know how long *that* will last. In about two days you'll start to hear, in a plaintive whine: "Mom, the puppy is biting me (stealing my toys, pooping on my homework, eating my homework)," "I have to do my homework so I don't have time to take him out," and so on. When you get a dog, you're acquiring a living, breathing being with huge needs. It's incredibly rewarding to raise a puppy, but be aware—it's not for the faint of heart.

Canine Caveats

An absolute cardinal rule: *Never* buy a dog for a child; buy a dog for *yourself*. If you're not willing or able to assume 100 percent responsibility for that dog, *don't get a dog!*

Feeding and Housetraining

What does it mean to add a puppy to your household, along with your existing children? First, it means feedings three to four times per day, and cleaning up messes several times per day for anywhere from a month or two to a year. Some dogs are house trained almost instantly and other puppies or dogs "just don't get it."

Since punishment will make the housetraining process only harder, there's nothing much you can do to "speed up the process." Just like toddlers, some puppies have the neurological development to "hold it" at an earlier age than others. You may get lucky and get one of the dogs who is house trained at 16 weeks, or you may get one that's simply incapable of being reliable until 10 or even 12 months of age.

Playtime

Be aware that the puppy's capacity for play is going to be *a lot* more than yours. He's going to be just like a pesky little kid who never wants to stop. This is normal and something that you, as the adult, need to accommodate.

Pooch Pointers

When dogs play, they body slam, growl, bite, and rearrange furniture. Dogs do *not* play Parcheesi. Puppies need vigorous play in order to develop into physically and mentally healthy dogs. While you can limit the venues and rules of the play, you must allow plenty of opportunities for it. If you get a puppy and want it to just sit on the corner and do nothing, he will never grow into a well-adjusted dog.

Proper Supervision and Doggie Daycare

It's a fact of life that puppies and dogs bite—it's natural and it's how they interact with their world, especially in the beginning. Human toddlers also go through a stage where they learn about their environment by putting things in their mouth.

You will have to constantly supervise any activity that includes children and your dog so that no one—dog or child—gets hurt. There will be accidents no matter how careful you are, and there will be some items that get chewed and some skin that gets nipped.

If you work full-time, you must find either a doggie daycare or a dog walker to come in several times per day. It's not unthinkable to get a puppy while you work full-time, but it's as cruel to leave a puppy all alone all day as it would be to leave a tiny infant alone all day. If you ask around, you'll find someone in your neighborhood who is available during the day and would be willing to baby-sit your pup. You can also find a doggie daycare for the first few months you have the puppy and then gradually leave the dog home for longer periods of time, while having a dog walker come in a few times.

Pooch Pointers

Some people "puppy proof" a room and then leave their pup loose in it, totally unsupervised. Such attempts generally fail. Think putting your puppy in a completely tiled bathroom is safe? Think again! You may find that he figures out how to chew the door or eat the linoleum floor.

Although crate training is essential, you can't expect a pup to stay in the crate all day. I recommend getting an exercise pen, also called an "X" pen. (You can get a pen from one of the pet supply mail-order catalogs for approximately $30 to $60, depending on the size.) You can put "safe" toys in it. If you're busy when you get home, at least you can put the puppy in it and he can move around a bit without getting into any trouble.

Teach Your Children

Okay, so you've decided that you *do* have the "stuff it takes"—the dedication, wherewithal, nerves of steel, patience of a saint, linoleum floors, stock in a paper-towel company, and the determination—to train this dog from day one so that he never ends up in a shelter.

Doggie Data

One of my students has a Rhodesian Ridgeback puppy, Liam, who loved to knock her three boys to the ground and sit on them. The boys didn't think that was funny, although the dog obviously did. We taught the boys to train the dog. Within two weeks, the dog stopped mauling them and was responding correctly to their cues for good behavior.

You've done extensive research and found a highly recommended breeder and bring home the puppy of your dreams (not, one hopes, the puppy of your nightmares).

Children as young as three and a half years old can be taught to train the dog along with you. This teaches the child responsibility, maturity, appreciation, and affection for a fellow creature. Having your child train your dog teaches the dog that kids are good things, but not chew toys or littermates. "The family that trains their dog together, enjoys their dog together."

(Photo by P. Dennison)

A five-year-old girl training her Boxer puppy to do sits.

R.E.S.P.E.C.T.

You can, should, and *must* train your children to respect your new dog as a living, breathing creature and not as a stuffed animal that can be replaced. Any child of any age should be taught to show consideration for the new family member.

If you can, bring your well-mannered children to puppy class and beginners class and have them train along with you. If the school doesn't allow children, teach them at home the exercises you learned in school.

Pooch Pointers _____

Please try not to look at training your dog as a chore. This should be a labor of love and just as important, if not more so, as taking your kids to soccer practice. The dog will learn many skills needed to make him a great adult, *and* you'll also have the family pet of your dreams.

Do's and Don'ts

Remember that TV commercial you saw with the happy puppies and giggling child that started this whole venture? Commercials are not real life and there are some very real do's and don'ts that have very serious ramifications if you mix them up.

Do's:

🏠 Supervise kids and dogs every second of every day.

🏠 Pair positives for the dog when the kids are around.

🏠 Reinforce your children for being nice to the dog.

🏠 Look for opportunities to reinforce the dog for tolerating rough handling by your kids.

🏠 Teach your kids to be calm and gentle.

🏠 Look at each new child you meet as a training opportunity, to continue the desensitization process.

Don'ts:

🏠 Never let your dog discipline your child. Watch your child to make sure he or she isn't being obnoxious to the dog. Watch your dog for signs of stress and call them away from each other if your dog gets nervous.

🏠 Never let your child discipline your dog. Remember that associative learning is happening all of the time. We certainly don't want your dog to have bad feelings toward your children.

🏠 Never leave your child and dog unsupervised.

🏠 Never let your children overstimulate the dog. Running around screaming in a high-pitched voice can actually stimulate prey drive. It's not fair to ask the dog to be calm under those circumstances *unless* you systematically desensitize him to screaming kids. Put the dog away if you're too busy to train him at that moment to accept the children.

Is it doable to have children and a dog? Of course it is, but don't bend to kid pressure or the American Dream pressure of having two and a half kids, two cars, a house, and a dog. Get a dog because *you* want one and have time for it for the next 15 to 17 years.

Pregnant Pause

You already have a dog and find out you're pregnant. Congratulations! As soon as you know you're expecting, you must start training your dog to accept the new baby. Don't wait until the baby is born to start desensitizing him—that's way too late.

Can you have a dog and a new baby? Yes, but you need to plan ahead and train ahead. If you don't have the dog yet and know you'll want a dog and a child, my wholehearted recommendation is to wait until your child is between five to eight years of age. In fact, most reputable breeders won't sell you a dog unless your kids are in this age group. And for good reason: We all know how hard it is to raise kids and dogs at the same time, and these breeders don't want their dogs to end up in a shelter or with behavior problems.

 Doggie Data

I heard a horror story once: A couple who was expecting their first child used a lifelike baby doll to play tug with their dog, thinking that would help the dog be calm around the baby. Do I have to spell out what happened?

Changes for the Dog

There are many things your dog will need to feel comfortable with when the new baby arrives. The more obvious ones are …

- 🏠 New smells.

- 🏠 Sights—baby doing baby things, plus all of the paraphernalia that goes along with a baby.

Doggie Data

Most of the dog bites in this country happen to small children, by their family's own dogs.

- 🏠 Sounds of crying and whining.

- 🏠 Baby things all over the house that aren't new chew toys.

The less obvious, but equally, if not more, important changes your dog can expect and for which you *must* train him to accept are …

- 🏠 Mommy and Daddy being cranky and tired and perhaps over-whelmed with the new baby.

- 🏠 Less attention, exercise, training, and petting than he's used to.

- 🏠 Being crated more often than he's used to.

- 🏠 The dog, himself, being cranky and tired because, of course, he'll get up every time you do to check on the baby.

- 🏠 Seeing a toddling baby and not mistaking the child for a prey object to be killed or played with roughly.

Protecting the Dog from Junior

Baby doesn't understand that your living, breathing dog is not a stuffed toy, and a four- or five-year-old child doesn't understand that the dog isn't a cartoon. Babies and young children don't have the cognitive capabilities to comprehend that the pain they inflict does, in fact, hurt. It's your job as the adult to make sure that the baby doesn't hurt the dog. An otherwise "nice" dog is extremely unlikely to hurt the baby, unless it is severely provoked.

Doggie Data

Mark's seven-year-old dog Cara was biting his one-year-old son in the face, and Mark was determined to work his dog through this. In a few weeks Cara learned to completely ignore the child. How? I taught Mark to watch Cara for signs of stress and to be more vigilant in watching both child and dog when they were out together. In addition, we taught Cara alternative behaviors, such as a "move away" cue, if the baby was bugging her. We also started to reinforce Cara heavily when the baby was around.

Preparing Your Dog for the Baby

So, what do you need to do the *instant* you find out you're pregnant? Train, train, train! Chaining your dog in the backyard for the rest of his life, or even for a brief time, is not an answer—ever.

Work on the foundation behaviors in Part 3, specifically eye contact, loose-leash walking, name recognition, come with distractions, long down stays (build up to about five minutes—approximate time it takes to change or feed a baby), proper door etiquette, *ignoring dropped food,* and accepting rough handling.

Doggie Data

One of the major differences between positive training and other methods is that the positive method builds a strong bond between you and the dog and teaches the dog that smaller, weaker things (like himself) are treated kindly and never physically or verbally corrected or punished. A dog trained this way is very likely to welcome the newest member of the household with a happy, nurturing spirit, because you taught him that small, helpless beings are to be cared for, not dominated. On the other hand, if you use punishment on your dog, he'll see that force is the way to control his environment and will be more likely to transfer that violence and ugly behavior onto the new baby.

Once the baby comes home, practice a lot of team training—where one of you feeds the baby and the other one reinforces the dog for being calm. You can train sit or down stays while diapering. Above all, make sure nothing bad happens to the dog in the presence of the baby.

You may even want to board the dog for a week when you first come home with the new baby. That way, once the dog comes home, you'll have gotten into a routine that you're comfortable with and can happily include the dog. Be sure that you've already boarded your dog a few times with a reputable kennel so that being kenneled will not be traumatic to him. You don't need him crazed when he comes home to you and the new baby.

Canine Caveats

Never punish your dog for being too rough or upset when the baby cries. Just calmly remind the dog to stay and give him something else to do. Watch him carefully, make sure he always remains calm, and reinforce any and all calm behaviors.

Having a child and a dog is not impossible and is in fact easy once you get the hang of it. Most of our childhood recollections include the dog we grew up with, so please feel free to let your children have those same great memories.

The Canine Bill of Rights

Your dog should have as many rights as your child. When you buy or rescue a dog, you're making a commitment to care for and train that dog to the best of your abilities for its lifetime. If you can't afford the time or money needed for health care and training, you may want to rethink getting a dog. When you take on the commitment, I hope you will promise to do the following:

- 🏠 Provide a place in your daily life for the 15+ years he will live, no matter what your life changes may be.

- 🏠 Provide quality food and clean water.

- 🏠 Provide proper socialization.

- 🏠 Provide shelter from hot and cold weather.

- 🏠 Provide clear, concise, *positive* training.

- 🏠 Provide good health care and regular grooming.

- 🏠 Provide daily physical exercise and mental stimulation and enrichment.

- 🏠 Provide the time and dedication to find proper solutions if the dog develops health or behavior problems.

In this throwaway society, our dogs seem to get the short end of the stick. They can't speak for themselves to tell us their requirements and fears, so we must anticipate and be aware of them. Dogs are social animals, as are humans. To make them live their lives alone in the backyard is like making you live in solitary confinement. You'd go crazy. I'm sure you know dogs that are isolated like this, who bark incessantly, lunge, pace, wear huge ruts in the dirt, and spend their lives alone with virtually no socialization, positive mental and physical stimulation, or companionship.

We owe it to our dogs to care for them in the best possible way. If you don't have time to train your dog, get a stuffed animal.

The Least You Need to Know

- 🏠 Avoid succumbing to "kid pressure" to get a dog if *you* aren't ready to take full responsibility.

- 🏠 Never punish your dog around your child—make positive associations only.

- 🏠 Teach your children to respect your dog and be vigilant in watching both of them.

- 🏠 The moment you find that you're pregnant, start training your dog to be ready for the changes the baby will bring.

- 🏠 You owe it to your dog to honor your lifetime commitment to him despite changes in your life.

Chapter

Solutions to "Bad" Behaviors

In This Chapter

- Are you accidentally reinforcing bad behaviors?
- "What's on top of the house?" (Roof!)
- Jumpin' Jack Flash
- Love at first bite
- Attention deficit dog disorder

I gotta tell you, I personally trained my own dogs to do all sorts of obnoxious behaviors before I knew better. I trained my Sheltie, Noel, to bark for four hours without taking a breath (you'd think dogs would get hoarse, wouldn't you?) and I also taught her to bark incessantly while I'm preparing her dinner. I taught my other Sheltie, Cody, to hate his dumbbell, and I allowed Cody to teach Beau and Shadow to fence chase (to run along the fence line while barking). Then I allowed Beau to teach Shadow and Mollie to counter surf (when the dog puts his paws up on the counter and "surfs" around, looking for the goodies you left for him).

Will I ever stop teaching my dogs "bad" behaviors? Probably not, because to err is human, and to forgive, canine. But I never blame the dogs because I know that I'm the one who trained them to do their "bad" behaviors. I stop it as soon as I see something happening and never let it get too far into "badness."

You, Too, Can Teach Your Dog Really Obnoxious Behaviors!

One of the hardest things to comprehend is that dogs are avid students and quickly learn *exactly* what we teach them. The problem is that we humans teach them the wrong behaviors! We don't do this on purpose, of course, but we do it nonetheless.

Canine Caveats

Behavior that's reinforced will be repeated. What you may not think of as being reinforcing—hitting, yelling, jerking the leash, attention for bad behaviors—is still *reinforcing for the dog*. If the only time you interact with your dog is to reprimand him, your dog will continue to do "bad" behaviors to get your attention.

Day after day, week after week, year after year, I see people *repeatedly reinforcing what they don't want!* Then they get angry at the dog, perhaps thinking that they have a stupid or stubborn dog. In reality, the dog is actually quite smart and is doing *exactly* what he was trained to do.

One Dog's Punishment Is Another's Reinforcement

It's not up to you to decide what's reinforcing (or punishing) to your dog—it's your dog's choice. One of my own dogs—Beau—*hates* tortellini and acts like I am trying to poison him, yet Cody would kill for tortellini. I've seen some dogs that love to be sprayed in the face with water and other dogs that find this very punishing.

If it suppresses behavior, it's a punishment. If it increases behavior, it's a reinforcer. Don't forget, though, that punishment only suppresses behavior; it doesn't eliminate it. It may stop the behavior for a short time, but the behavior always comes back at one time or another.

What Behavior Do You Want?

First of all, you must know the exact behavior you really want. Sounds simple doesn't it? But most people are so angry or upset and focused on their dog's "bad" behaviors that they can't think clearly.

Try not to concentrate on the behavior you don't want—really *think* about what you want to the dog to do *instead*. Make a list of all the behaviors the dog does that you don't like, in one column. Then in another column, write down the behaviors that you would prefer the dog to do. (See Chapter 2 for a sample chart.) Once you have your list, you'll know exactly what you want. Then reinforce only the "good" behaviors.

The following sections discuss some of the behaviors that are probably on your list and what you can do about them.

Pooch Pointers

My preference is to reinforce "good" behaviors that are incompatible with "bad" ones. For instance, sitting is incompatible with jumping. Have an active dog that climbs the walls? Lying down is incompatible with rearranging the furniture.

Bark! Bark! Bark!

Your dog barks incessantly and you ignore him up to a point. Then *you* start barking (yelling) along with the dog, thus reinforcing the dog's barking. Yahoo! Barking is a very hard behavior to stop because there are so many triggers for it. Real or imagined noises, sights, smells, other animals, kids, and fast movements are just a few of the eight zillion prompts for barking.

Why Dogs Bark

Some dogs learn to use barking to get your attention. Many dogs bark because (it seems, anyway) they like to hear themselves talk. Shetland Sheepdogs bark at the footfall of a squirrel from two days ago. Some dogs bark out of stress, arousal, or even boredom (which can also be stressful). And some breeds, such as Beagles, Akbash, Great Pyrenees, Anatolian Shepherd Dogs, and Lhasa Apsos, were specifically bred to bark as part of their jobs (such as herding, hunting, and guarding).

Barking Solutions

As hard as this may seem, the best thing to do is to completely ignore the dog. Walk out of the room, put earplugs in, do whatever you have to do to not react to your dog. Then after five seconds to five minutes of no barking (depending on the length of time the dog was barking), reinforce the dog for the quiet behavior. The longer the dog barks, the longer the quiet behavior should be. Reinforce too soon after five minutes of barking and that will be what you'll get more of.

If you give in and respond to the dog's barking after, let's say, three minutes, you've just reinforced three minutes of barking. If you then try again and blow your cool after 10 minutes, you've now reinforced 10 minutes of barking. You get the picture.

You can set the dog up not to bark. Let's say when you walk into the vet's office, your dog barks. So stop him from barking before you get to the door. Keep his focus on you by using treats as you walk up to the door. (Practice your door etiquette beforehand—see Chapter 12.) As soon as you're both in the door, re-engage his focus and heavily reward him for paying attention to you. Keep him busy with silly pet tricks while you're in the waiting room.

Canine Caveats

Reducing or even eliminating barking from the dog's behavior repertoire is not impossible; it just isn't the easiest "bad" behavior to get rid of—especially if you've been reinforcing it in the past.

No matter the situation, as long as you know your dog will react, set him up to be quiet. If he barks in crowds, stay farther away and reinforce quiet behaviors. If he barks at kids running, enlist the neighborhood kids to help you. Have them walk by slowly, reinforcing your dog for not barking. Then have them slowly jog by, then run by, then maybe even add that ear-piercing scream that most kids know how to do, all the while reinforcing your dog for quiet behaviors.

Start these progressions at a large distance and then gradually decrease the distance. If at any time your dog barks, do not reinforce him by comforting him, yelling at him, or jerking the leash. Just wait until he calms down for at least five seconds, give him something else to do, and then reinforce for quiet behaviors.

Pogo Stick Revisited: Jumping

Say your dog jumps on people coming to the door. Dogs jump to greet people—it is a natural submissive greeting behavior and they have to jump because we're taller than they are. Oddly enough (from a human standpoint), the dog thinks that, by offering these submissive behaviors, he's being very polite.

Pooch Pointers

Contrary to old-fashioned beliefs, jumping up is not a sign of dominance or aggression.

Reactions to Jumping

Half of the people will pet the dog, reinforcing the dog for jumping. You've heard them, "Oh it's okay, I love dogs." The other half will yank the dog down, squeeze his paws until he is screaming in pain, or knee him in the chest. Or you may yank the dog down or yell at him.

All of these reactions reinforce the dog for jumping—including the negative reactions. Punish the dog for jumping and he may feel the need to jump even more in a submissive, frantic manner to appease your anger, increasing the cycle of jumping on people. Or the dog may decide that people are dangerous (since so much punishment happens around people) and, as you have learned in previous chapters, the jumping may intensify into fearful biting behaviors or extreme shyness.

Jumping to Solutions

These are some of my favorite options you can adopt to teach your dog that "four on the floor" is more rewarding for him:

- Avert your eyes and turn sideways as he's about to jump—you can always see the signs in their little eyes or in their bodies! If you miss the signals and the dog jumps, still turn sideways to deflect the dog. Then once he has four on the floor, wait passively for five seconds ask him to "Sit" and then reinforce.

- You can also walk away slowly (a calming signal) and reinforce the dog for staying on the ground. Throw treats on the floor to further reinforce that "down there" is better. Play the "rev up and cool down" game in Chapter 10.

- Become a tree stump. Don't move. After all, how reinforcing can a tree stump be? Don't look at the dog and don't talk to the dog or push him away. Trees don't have eyes, ears, mouths, or arms. Just stand there. He'll eventually get down. Wait for five seconds, ask him to "Sit" and then reinforce.

- Teach the dog to jump on cue by encouraging him to jump and saying "Up" when he does. Give him a quick pet and murmur "Good." Then look away and become a stump. *When* you feel the dog get off, say "Off" and have a party! Give him the jackpot of his life—tons of food, calm petting, praise, and lots of attention. Repeat a billion times. He'll soon learn that the reward for not jumping is infinitely better than the reward for jumping.

- One of my favorite options is to teach the dog to "Go Visit." "Go Visit" means that *on your command only*, the dog goes up to the person you're pointing at and lies down! (Lying down is incompatible with jumping.)

🏠 If your dog jumps wildly on people coming to the door, make the doorbell a cue to go to his crate. Or teach the dog that a person approaching is a cue to sit or lie down and heavily reinforce it.

Doggie Data _____

Mark came in with his five-month-old Boxer, Merlin, and his four and a half-year-old daughter Jean. Merlin was body-slamming Jean to the ground on a daily basis. Within one hour, Merlin stopped knocking Jean over, and it has lasted two years so far. Was it magic?

Nope—I just taught Jean to use head turns, body turns, and walking away slowly to reinforce Merlin for being on the ground. The relationship between the two has improved so much so that now Jean is the main trainer of the dog! If a four and a half-year-old child can do it, so can you!

Fluffy, Can I Have My Arm Back Now?

"Ouch! There he goes again! Stop it. *Stop it. I said stop it!* This dog is driving me crazy!" Sound familiar? Biting, like jumping, can be inadvertently reinforced by your actions. In fact, the cures for biting are very similar to those for jumping.

Dogs bite for many reasons: Because they can, because that's how they play with other dogs, because they get a "rise" out of us, and because it's fun.

Pooch Pointers _____

When was the last time your dog got together with Muffy from down the street to play Parcheesi? Not in your recent memory? Maybe they do when all the humans are sleeping? I think not. Dogs play by biting, body slamming, chasing, humping, growling, barking, and knocking over furniture. This is normal dog play behavior. It's not aggression—even if the play is directed at you.

Quit Biting!

If your dog bites you or mouths you, use the calming signals you learned in Chapters 7 and 8—turn sideways, yawn, move slowly away, or sit or lie down (if possible without being further mauled).

Watch for any patterns of when the biting or mouthing behaviors start. Is it a certain time of day, are you ignoring the dog, or are you overexciting the dog with too rough play? Is the dog underexercised, overfed, or bored?

If he bites you at a certain time of day or when you are too busy to pay attention to him, you have two options: You can start engaging him in play *before* he starts, or you can completely walk away and ignore him. Put a barrier between you if necessary or go into another room and shut the door. You must be silent however, and you can't be silent when you're in pain, so this should be a good incentive for you to watch your dog and stop the biting behavior before it starts!

Pooch Pointers

If your dog bites because you're trying to handle or groom him, review the handling guide in Chapter 11.

If your dog is underexercised and overfed, well, you know what you have to do. Get up off the couch and go outside and have a party. Walking sedately around the block on a six-foot leash is not enough aerobic exercise for the normal dog. He needs running, swimming, chasing toys, hiking, long walks in the woods, and whatever else you can think of that your dog likes.

Pooch Pointers

When you're feeling lazy after a hard day, repeat after me, "A tired dog is a good dog." I don't know about you, but I really love to see my dogs having such a good time, knowing that I'm able to make those fun things possible. Is that egotistical? Maybe, but *my* dogs are good dogs! I'll have plenty of time to lie around and watch TV in my next life.

You may be stressing out your dog by playing too rough with him. You get rougher and he doesn't know how to get you to stop, so he bites you. Should you be angry? *Not!* You're the one who pushed him too far. If this is happening to you, you have some choices. Stop roughhousing with the dog and use toys instead. Or if you insist on playing with him with your not-puncture-resistant arms and hands, stop the play before your dog gets too aroused or stressed. Then pet him lightly and gently to calm him down completely.

Biting the Kids

Does your dog chase and bite kids who are running? Then desensitize your dog to running kids and teach the dog to ignore them. Or teach the kids to play the "rev up and cool down" game with the dog. Or use better judgment and don't let the dog be around the kids when they're acting like screaming banshees.

Perhaps your dog bites your kids for inappropriate petting (on the head and back-of-neck areas). So teach them how to pet the dog so he doesn't feel threatened (review Chapter 11) *and* teach the dog to accept inappropriate petting.

If you have a youngster toddling around, teach your dog to accept pinching and hair pulling. Pinch, click and treat for no reaction, then pull, click and treat for no reaction. Don't start out by yanking the dog off his feet—start out lightly and gradually build to harder pinches (although not so hard as to bruise him).

Can Dogs Really Have ADD?

Of course dogs can have attention deficit disorder—if you train it! Let's say you want to train your dog and he ignores you, or he has "selective deafness." You cheerlead and possibly bribe with a treat to try to get the dog's attention. When he finally does come to you, you may play with him or give him a treat. Your dog now ignores you more and more for longer and longer periods of time. What were you really reinforcing? The inattention!

> **Doggie Data** _____
>
> Fran came in with her Golden Retriever, Dexter, for lessons. Dexter had a really bad case of ADD and would ignore Fran about 99 percent of the time. I put them on a "work for a living" program and the results were astounding. Fran was so pleased with Dexter's newfound focus in just one week, that she continued to feed Dexter all of his meals from her hand for "jobs."

Go back to the basics from Chapter 10: eye contact, name, recall word, and praise word recognition.

Hand feed the dog for two weeks—not for free, but for specific behaviors such as sits, downs, eye contact, or anything the dog knows how to do. You can "insist" on eye contact going through doors, in and out of the car, in and out of the crate, and from one location to another. Follow these steps:

1. Wait for 30 seconds for the dog to give you eye contact. If he doesn't give you eye contact (with no verbal prodding from you), the dog gets a trip back to the crate (with no emotion from you; you should periodically give the dog a treat for going back in the crate—yes, even for "failing").

2. Repeat again and again until you get eye contact within 30 seconds.

3. Next, raise your criteria and now wait for only 25 seconds before sending the dog back to his crate. Repeat again and again until you get eye contact within 25 seconds.

4. Then raise your criteria and lower the amount of time you wait for eye contact.

5. Keep repeating until you get eye contact within three seconds.

Once your dog is looking at you within three seconds, you can start working on whatever behaviors you want. If you lose the dog's attention, wait three seconds to see whether you can get it back (again, no verbal prompting from you). If not, back to the crate he goes.

Most people find this process takes a few weeks or months—depending on how long they've reinforced the dog's inattention. Don't lower your criteria just because you want to train for a specific amount of time or have some other goal in mind. If you do, you'll shoot yourself in the foot by starting the cycle of inattention again. Attention is the foundation of all training and should never be taken for granted.

The Least You Need to Know

- Every time you yell at your dog, hit him, or punish him in any way for barking, jumping, or biting, you're reinforcing those behaviors.

- If you make an "issue" of jumping and biting, they will become rock-solid behaviors.

- Concentrate on teaching your dog alternate behaviors and watch him carefully for signs that you are pushing him too hard.

- If you aren't ignoring a bad behavior, you're reinforcing it.

Chapter 19

Incorporating Training into Your Life

In This Chapter

- Fifteen minutes a day
- Stop exercising and the muscle will turn to flab
- Don't miss the easy opportunities to train
- A whole new world

I'm sure you are wondering how the heck you're supposed to train your dog when you work full-time. With a little planning on your part, you can easily accomplish it. The charts and tips in this chapter will show you the way. Then you'll get a preview of some of the fun training activities you and your dog can participate in down the road.

Consistent Training and Variable Reinforcements Are the Key

When athletes train, they are consistent and dedicated. They know that if they put off training, they'll lose their skills. Dog training is *not*

like riding a bike—your dog *will* forget his new behaviors if they aren't practiced. Give yourself a break and *you* will lose the desire to continue.

While you do have to consistently set aside some time each and every day to spend some quality time training your friend, you should vary the frequency and type of reinforcement given during those sessions. But don't confuse "consistency in training" with being variable and unpredictable in how you reinforce.

An Exercise in Creative Reinforcements

If it's hard for you to be creative in how you set up your training sessions, you can try this: Write 5 to 10 or more behaviors on separate slips of paper. Here are some examples of behaviors to use:

- Sit
- Backups (make different slips each for no distractions, mild distractions, and lots of distractions)
- Sit stay (10 and 20 seconds)
- Down
- Loose-leash walking (with no distractions, mild distractions, and lots of distractions)
- Down stay (10 and 20 seconds)
- Shake paw
- Sit politely for petting (by you and by someone else)
- Rollover
- Settle (with and without handling)
- Door etiquette in the house, car, and vet's office
- Come (with no distractions, mild distractions, and lots of distractions)
- Stand
- Stand stay (with and without touching)

Fold up the slips and put them in a hat. Every day, pick three behaviors out of the hat and that's what you work on for that day. At the end of the day, put those slips back into the hat to be used again. As your dog's skill level goes up, exchange the slips for more difficult behaviors. These don't have to be all that complicated—just pick things that will stimulate his brain. A few examples:

- Hide a treat or toy in a blanket or towel and encourage the dog to "find it." This encourages him to use his nose—great for scent-discrimination exercises for more advanced training.

- Show him a toy, tell him to stay, and then hide the toy (in plain sight at first). Then release him to "find it." You can gradually make your hiding places harder and harder.

- Teach him to touch his nose to a target—such as your hand or a plastic lid. Nose targeting is great for many things—it teaches the dog to turn his head away from another dog to avoid potential problems (head turning is a calming signal). Targeting a plastic lid is great for when you're teaching some of the obstacles in agility training.

- Get a Kong toy and fill it with gooey things and some hard treats that are slightly bigger than the opening. This will give him a little mental puzzle to keep him happy and busy. (Kongs are heavy-duty rubber toys with a hollow center to stuff things in.)

There are many simple ways to add enrichment and variability to your dog's life without going too crazy. You can even teach him service dog behaviors, such as picking up keys—or better yet—*finding* keys, closing cabinet doors (I wouldn't recommend teaching him to open cabinet doors), or retrieving your slippers.

Training Goals

No one is ever done with training, but there are some behaviors you should strive for, as recommended by noted positive trainer Ted Turner. Teach all of these and you will be the envy of every other dog owner you meet!

- Eye contact
- Name recognition
- Praise-word recognition
- Walking on a loose leash
- Walking on a loose leash with attention to you
- Accepting petting, handling, and grooming
- Stays (with distractions)
- Recall (with distractions)
- Crate training
- Control in/out of doorways and cars
- Potty training
- Allows food removal and ignores dropped food
- No aggression to humans or dogs
- No jumping, mouthing, or biting
- Tolerance of children
- Not totally reliant on food as a reinforcer

Please don't think that these are unattainable—they aren't. It just takes consistency, patience, specific goals on your part, and faith that your dog—yes, *your* dog—can achieve this level of training.

Incorporating Training into Your Routine

I know it's hard sometimes to think about training your dog when you come home tired, but you owe it to yourself and to your dog. After all, why else did you get a dog if not to have fun with him? Once you "just do it," you should find your energy level actually increases and your mental state improves. After all, it has been proven that when hospital or nursing-home patients are around dogs, they're happier and more relaxed.

You can train your dog almost any time of the day or night—while you cook, eat, clean, talk on the phone, work on the computer, watch TV, run errands, go to the softball game, go swimming, take a hike, or ride a bike.

A typical day of running errands and training at the same time can be the following:

Canine Caveats

When running errands while training your dog, be sure to watch the weather. In even relatively mild weather (65 degrees and above) a dog, can die of heatstroke in six minutes if left in a closed and unprotected car. Even if he doesn't die, he can suffer irreparable brain damage.

🐾 Go to the bank, bring the dog with you, and practice door etiquette.

🐾 Pick up your dry cleaning and practice loose-leash walking in the parking lot.

🐾 While doing your laundry at the Laundromat, practice stays and eye contact and play hide the cookie or toy in the towel game. You can even put the dog on a longer leash and practice recalls.

🐾 When you go to the pet shop, practice door etiquette, sitting politely for petting, and loose-leash walking.

So you see, it's not hard to find time to work with your dog. My hope for you is that you become a training junkie and sell your couch and TV to make room for training equipment!

An Apple a Day

If you spend as little as three five-minute sessions per day training your dog, you'll have a good dog. The sessions don't have to be strictly formal—you can train your dog while running errands or doing chores around the house. You can (and should) train while you play with him and play while you train. Your dog should not know the difference between playing and training—both should be equally fun and satisfying. What may actually happen is that you end up

> **Doggie Data**
>
> Bobbi grumbled about one of the charts that showed how to train while cleaning. Her complaint? "But that means I have to clean!"

enjoying the sessions because your dog soaks up whatever you teach him. You'll see positive results and that will spur you on to train more.

Following the training charts in this section will …

- 🐾 Keep you on track with each new behavior.

- 🐾 Advance each behavior in small approximations (steps).

- 🐾 Help you to become variable in how you reinforce.

- 🐾 Give you an idea of how you can train your dog, even while cleaning the house.

Sample Training Guides

These charts are a checklist and guideline for training. They list the many different behaviors you can work on, plus how you can be variable and unpredictable in how you reinforce each repetition. Once you get the hang of this, you can make up your own charts based on the behaviors your dog still needs to learn.

WEEK ONE

Monday

Sit
___ 2 treats
___ 5 treats
___ pets & praise
___ 1 treat & pet
___ ball toss

Backups
___ 10 treats
___ 1 treat
___ ball toss
___ 4 treats
___ pets & praise
___ 6 treats

Eye Contact
___ 1 treat
___ 4 treats
___ pets & praise
___ 2 treats
___ 1 treat
___ run away silly
___ 4 treats

Come, click & treat
For 5 minutes

Sit
___ 2 treats
___ 3 treats
___ pet & 1 treat
___ praise
___ 5 treats

Eye Contact
___ 1 treat
___ 2 treats
___ ball toss
___ praise
___ petting
___ 5 treats

Tuesday

Down
___ 10 treats
___ pet and 2 treats
___ ball toss
___ 1 treat
___ 4 treats

Eye contact
___ pets & praise
___ 3 treats
___ 1 treat
___ pet & ball toss
___ 1 treat
___ 1 treat

Sit
___ praise
___ 1 treat
___ ball toss
___ run away silly
___ 4 treats
___ pet & 3 treats
___ pet

Backups
___ 1 treat
___ 1 treat
___ 6 treats
___ run away silly
___ 2 treats
___ pets & praise

Come, click & treat
for 2 minutes

Down
___ 5 treats
___ 2 treats
___ pets & praise
___ pets & 8 treats
___ pets and water

Wednesday

Eye contact
___ 1 treat
___ 2 treats
___ pets & praise
___ pet & 1 treat
___ 1 treat

Name, click, treat
For 5 minutes

Cuddle time

Down
___ 9 treats
___ 3 treats
___ ball toss
___ run away silly

Sit
___ praise
___ Praise and pets
___ 4 treats
___ 1 treat

**Sit before you
throw the toy.**

**Down before you
throw the toy.**

Name, click & treat
for 5 minutes

Backups
___ 1 treat
___ 1 treat
___ 4 treats

Thursday

Cuddle time

Come, click & treat
For 5 minutes

Name, click & treat
for 5 minutes

Sit for toy tosses

Down for toy tosses

**Eye contact for
toy tosses**

Stand
___ 1 treat
___ 2 treats
___ 1 treat
___ 5 treats

Cuddle time

Eye contact for petting

Sit
___ 1 treat
___ hand clapping
___ run away silly
___ ball toss
___ 4 treats

Friday

Stand
___ 3 treats
___ gentle petting
___ 1 treat
___ 5 treats

Eye contact, click & treat
for 3 minutes

**Put leash on, click
and treat. Then take
leash off, click and
treat – repeat 10 times**

Backups
___ 4 treats
___ petting
___ Praise
___ 7 treats
___ 1 treat

**Hide & Seek – praise,
treats and petting**
___ in the bathroom
___ in the bedroom
___ in the closet
___ in the kitchen

**Touch top of head
game – repeat 10 times,
clicking & treating for
no movement away**

Cuddle time

Saturday

**Go to a field
and play with dog
on a 50-foot long line**

While playing, add in:

**Eye contact, click
& treat for 2 minutes**

**Name, click &
treat for 3 minutes**

3 sits
___ 3 treats
___ petting
___ 1 treat

4 downs
___ petting
___ praise
___ 5 treats

Backups
___ 6 treats
___ praise
___ 1 treat
___ ball toss

**Once at home,
Put leash on, click
and treat. Then take
leash off, click and
treat – repeat 10 times**

**Touch top of head and
neck areas – repeat 10
times, clicking & treating
for no movement away.**

Week one training guide. (Designed by P. Dennison)

WEEK TWO

Monday	Tuesday	Wednesday	Thursday	Friday	Saturday
Sit ___ 1 treats ___ 7 treats ___ pets & praise ___ 1 treat & pet ___ ball toss	**Down** ___ 10 treats ___ pet and 2 treats ___ ball toss ___ 1 treat ___ 4 treats	**Throw the cookie game** ___ 10 treats ___ 12 treats ___ pets & praise ___ pet & 1 treat ___ 7 treats	**Eye contact** ___ 1 treat ___ petting ___ praise ___ 8 treats	**"Shamu" down stays** ___ 10 seconds ___ 18 seconds ___ 18 seconds	Go to a field and play with dog on a 50-foot long line
Stand stay ___ 1 second ___ 2 seconds ___ 3 seconds ___ 4 seconds ___ 5 seconds ___ 6 seconds	**"Shamu" Down stay** ___ 3 seconds ___ 3 seconds **play for 4 minutes** **"Shamu" Down stay** ___ 3 seconds ___ 4 seconds ___ 4 seconds	**"Shamu" down stay** ___ 4 seconds ___ 6 seconds ___ 6 seconds **Name, click, treat** For 5 minutes	**Come, click & treat** For 5 minutes **Throw the cookie game** ___ 6 treats ___ 8 treats ___ 10 treats ___ petting & 11 treats	**Eye contact, click & treat for 3 minutes**	While playing, add in: The two toy game and the two tug game. Be sure to play by your rules.
Eye Contact ___ 1 treat ___ 1 treat ___ pets & praise ___ 2 treats ___ 1 treat ___ run away silly ___ 4 treats	**Sit** ___ praise ___ 1 treat ___ ball toss ___ run away silly ___ 4 treats ___ pet & 3 treats ___ pet	**Stand for touching** ___ 4 treats ___ 3 treats ___ 5 treats	**Cuddle time**	**Put leash on, click and treat. Then take leash off, click and treat – repeat 10 times**	**Name, click & treat for 3 minutes**
Come, click & treat For 5 minutes	**Backups w/distractions** ___ 4 treats ___ 2 treat ___ 6 treats ___ run away silly ___ 2 treats ___ pets & praise	**Sit for toy tosses** **Eye contact for toy tosses**	**"Shamu" Down stay** ___ 6 seconds ___ 10 seconds ___ 10 seconds	**Backups w/ distractions** ___ 4 treats ___ petting ___ run away silly ___ 7 treats ___ 1 treat	Backups or perhaps loose leash walking if your dog is focused on you.
Stand w/touching ___ 1 treats ___ 2 treats ___ pet & 1 treat ___ praise ___ 5 treats		**Sit** ___ praise ___ Praise and pets ___ 4 treats ___ 1 treat ___ run away silly	**Eye contact for toy tosses** **Stand stay** ___ 1 treat ___ 2 treats ___ 5 treats	**Hide & Seek – praise, treats and petting** ___ in the bathroom ___ in the bedroom ___ in the closet ___ in the kitchen	Teach your dog how to shake paw **"Shamu" down stays** ___ 18 seconds ___ 34 seconds ___ 34 seconds
Name, click & treat for 3 minutes	**Come, click & treat or 2 minutes**	**Practice door etiquette** **Practice food bowl etiquette** **Name, click & treat for 5 minutes**	**Cuddle time** **Eye contact for petting** Put leash on, click and treat. Then take leash off, click and treat – repeat 10 times	**Touch top of head game** – repeat 10 times, clicking & treating for no movement away **Cuddle time** **Play fetch for eye contact, sits and downs**	Once at home, Put leash on, click and treat. Then take leash off, click and treat – repeat 10 times Cuddle time

Week two training guide. (Designed by P. Dennison)

WEEK THREE

Monday	Tuesday	Wednesday	Thursday	Friday	Saturday
Drop the cookie game	**Door etiquette**	**Real Life**	**Settle**	**Teach your dog to roll over**	Show off to your friends all you have taught your dog in ONLY 3 weeks! Congratulations!!!
___ 1 treat	___ front door	___ 2 toy game	___ 1 treat		
___ 7 treats	___ back door	___ while dusting	___ light petting	**Name, click & treat for 3 minutes**	**Loose leash walking for 5 steps**
___ pets & praise	___ side door	___ down stay while doing dishes	___ 3 treats		
___ 2 tug games			___ 6 treats	**Stand stay**	___ Sit
___ 4 treats	**"Shamu" Down stay**	___ down stay while vacuuming	**Name, click & treat**	___ for head touch	
	___ 66 seconds	___ throw the cookie game while working on computer	**For 5 minutes**	___ for tail touch	___ Down
Loose-leash walking				___ for paw touch	
___ 1 step (C/T)	**Stand stay for petting**		**Drop the cookie game**		___ Down stay for 66 seconds
___ 1 step (C/T)	___ head	**Loose leash walking**	___ petting	**Loose leash walking**	
___ 1 step (C/T)	___ shoulder	___ 3 steps (C/T)	___ praise & 8 treats	___ 4 steps (C/T)	___ Stand & stay for handling
___ 1 step (C/T)	___ back	___ 3 steps (C/T)	___ 6 treats	___ 5 steps (C/T)	
___ 1 step (C/T)	___ head	___ 3 steps (C/T)	___ petting & 3 treats	___ 5 steps (C/T)	___ Shake paw and wave
		___ 3 steps (C/T)		___ 5 steps (C/T)	
"Shamu" down stays	**Sit**	___ 3 steps (C/T)	**Settle with a stay**	___ 5 steps (C/T)	___ Settle
___ 34 seconds	___ praise		___ 9 treats		
___ 34 seconds	___ ball toss	**Name, click, treat**	___ 3 treats	**2 tug game –**	___ Roll over
___ 66 seconds	___ run away silly	**For 5 minutes**	___ 1 treat	don't forget the rules! Add in a sit or down before allowing the dog to retake the toy.	
	___ pet & 3 treats		___ light petting		___ Name recognition
Practice "Shake paw"	___ pet	**Door etiquette**	___ 5 treats		
		___ in the car			___ Come word recognition
Cuddle time	**Loose-leash walking**	___ coming out of car	**"Shamu" Down stay**	**"Shamu" sit stays**	
	___ 1 step (C/T)	___ at the post office	___ 66 seconds	___ 3 seconds	___ Door etiquette
Name, click & treat for 3 minutes	___ 2 steps (C/T)	___ at the bank	___ 66 seconds	___ 3 seconds	
	___ 2 steps (C/T)	___ at the Laundromat		___ 3 seconds	___ Staying still for petting
Food bowl etiquette	___ 2 steps (C/T)		**Sits for toy tosses**		
	___ 2 steps (C/T)	**Cuddle time**	___ for paw touches	**Cuddle time**	___ Not leaving you even if the leash is off, until you release the dog
Water bowl etiquette	___ 2 steps (C/T)		___ for paw touches		
		Teach your dog to "wave"	___ for head touch	**Sit still while you brush for treats. Keep it slow – 1 brush stroke at a time. Continue in this vein, adding more and more brushing. Have someone help you by feeding it dog is still.**	___ Fetch games for eye contact, sits and downs
Sit	**Have someone hold your dog's leash, while you call the dog. Make sure they drop the leash as soon as you say "come." As reinforcers, use food, petting, praise, runaway silly, and toys**	**Bonus points if you teach the dog to shake and wave with both paws!**	___ for leaning over in an obnoxious way		
___ 4 treats					
___ 1 treat		**Settle**	**Eye contact for petting & toy toss**		
___ petting		___ 5 treats			
___ praise		___ 3 treats	**Put leash on, click and treat. Then take leash off, click and treat – repeat 10 times**		
		___ 4 treats			
		___ 1 treat			
		___ run away silly			

Week three training guide. (Designed by P. Dennison)

As you can see, this is all pretty basic stuff that will fit easily into your busy schedule. You'll notice that, in the beginning, lots of food is used, but as the weeks go on, other types of reinforcers are used to keep the behaviors intact.

Where All This Fun Might Lead You

Okay, so now you're completely and utterly hooked on dog training. Your dog is doing incredible behaviors and you want *more!* Good for you—and great for your dog! Never fear, there are plenty of additional activities you can do with your dog.

Canine Good Citizen (CGC)

Once you have achieved basic training, training your dog to earn the Canine Good Citizen title is your next step. This title and certificate are offered by the American Kennel Club (AKC). When your dog becomes a Canine Good Citizen, he is recognized for being well-behaved at home, in public, and around other dogs. This title is available to any dog, regardless of breed. Mixed breeds are also encouraged to participate.

The CGC test includes 10 tests. They include being calm while a stranger approaches, sitting politely for petting, allowing a stranger to lightly brush and examine ears and feet, "Sit" and "Down" on command, "Stay" while you walk 20 feet away, a recall from 10 feet away, loose-leash walking, walking through a crowd, reactions to a noise and sight distraction, and supervised separation, where you go away for three minutes while someone holds the leash.

Don't worry if you don't pass it the first time. You're allowed to take it as many times as you wish and the feeling of accomplishment is wonderful!

Therapy Dog

Most hospitals, nursing homes, and schools welcome Therapy Dogs. The primary objective for a Therapy Dog is to provide comfort and companionship to patients. The dogs increase emotional well-being, promote healing, and improve the quality of life for the people they visit.

For your dog to be a registered Therapy Dog, he must first pass his Canine Good Citizen test, as well as be trained to ignore dropped food (not really as hard as you may think!) and be calm around wheelchairs, walkers, and canes. In addition, the dog needs to be relaxed around people walking erratically and be willing to be handled by strangers and to actively seek out petting. Your dog must be at least one year old to take the test.

> **Doggie Data**
>
> I used to take some of my dogs to a nursing home. One time, a nurse asked me if I could put Noel in bed with a woman who had been comatose for many years. When I did, the nurse took the woman's hand and had her gently pet Noel. Within seconds there was a definite positive reaction from the patient.

There are many organizations that you can register with to enable your dog to become a Therapy Dog. They generally offer insurance (in case your dog accidentally hurts someone) that is usually quite inexpensive. The Delta Society and Therapy Dog International are the two largest organizations. If your dog is not registered with a group, you will not be allowed to enter hospitals or nursing homes with him.

Rally-O

This is a new sport that's a natural steppingstone from the CGC to competition obedience or agility (see the following sections for more on these dog sports). Many of the maneuvers are similar to competition obedience, but you can talk to your dog the entire time while giving extra cues. You follow a course of signs and do the behavior listed on the sign, rather than respond to a judge's commands as you would in competition obedience.

Rally-O is a great way to acclimate you and your dog to the "show scene" in a fun, exciting, and nonscary way. The scoring is less stringent than competition obedience and is great for the trainer who isn't quite sure what he or she wants to do next. Train for Rally-O and you can go on to competition obedience or agility with ease.

At this time, Rally-O is offered as a nonregular class at many sanctioned AKC dog shows. The Association of Pet Dog Trainers (APDT) does offer titles in Rally-O. I expect that the AKC will soon offer titles as well.

Competition Obedience

Competition obedience is the foundation upon which all other dog sports are based. Training for competition develops a strong working relationship between the dog and his owner. A few of the behaviors you dog must master to earn the three main titles are heeling on and off leash at different paces, standing still while a stranger lightly examines the dog, sit and down stays in a group of other dogs, dumbbell retrieves, jumping, and scent discrimination.

There are three main levels of obedience competition: Novice, Open, and Utility. You can also train for and earn an Obedience Trial Champion (OTCH) title. The levels increase in complexity and really hone your skills as a trainer. Any one of the titles says a great deal about you and your dog, your relationship, and your dedication. Your dog can wear these titles proudly!

There are three main registries that promote competition obedience. The AKC allows only purebred dogs to compete in its trials. The United Kennel Club (UKC) allows mixed-breed dogs to enter, and the Australian Shepherd Club of America (ASCA) allows any breed as well as mixed breeds to compete in its trials. The American Mixed Breed Obedience Registry (AMBOR) is only for mixed breeds.

Agility

Very simply, agility is an obstacle course for dogs. Your dog must follow the course correctly, accurately, safely, and *fast!* There are many levels and types of classes offered that will fit into most people's and dog's abilities.

Agility is fun and challenging to both dog and handler. The AKC offers agility trials (purebred dogs only) as do the North American Agility Council (NADAC) and United States Dog Agility Association (USDAA). These last two registries allow purebred and mixed-breed dogs to compete.

Sheep Herding

You can train for sheep herding with just about any breed of dog that has any "sheep sense." I've even seen Standard Poodles and German Shorthaired Pointers do a fine job herding sheep. However, if you want to actually compete, you can do so only with a breed of dog that the AKC classifies as part of the Herding group (for example, Border Collies, Old English Sheepdogs, and Corgis). The AKC and ASCA are the two registries that hold herding trials. There are also many trials for Border Collies only.

Other Sports

There are additional dog sports for many other breeds, such as tracking, search and rescue, carting (pulling a cart), weight pull, flyball (a timed relay race, with a team of four dogs jumping over four hurdles, taking a tennis ball out of a "flyball box," and jumping back over the four hurdles), earthdog (or "go to ground," where terriers find the rodents that are caged underground), lure coursing (chasing a "lure" through a prescribed course), conformation (a beauty contest for purebred dogs—think "Westminster Kennel Club dog show"), water sports, and water rescue.

For more information, see Appendix B. Each of these sports has a personality of its own. You will meet some wonderful people and develop great new friendships, which will change your life—and your dog's—for the better.

The Least You Need to Know

- Train a few minutes every day and you will have a great dog.
- Use the places on your daily errand list as opportunities to train your dog.
- Lay down your dog's foundation behaviors and the sky's the limit to what you can accomplish.
- Get involved with some dog sports and make new friends.

Appendix **A**

Glossary

adrenaline and **glucocorticoids**   Hormones that are produced in mammals during stress to help the body prepare for a fight-or-flight response.

alpha   The dog in charge. Very often people misinterpret which dog is alpha, incorrectly thinking that the bully or the most aggressive dog is the "alpha" dog.

alpha roll   Grappling a dog to the ground and holding him in a submissive position.

antecedent   A cue, or something that comes before a behavior.

approximations   Small steps that make up a final behavior.

arcing   A behavior dogs exhibit when they meet. Rather than going straight up to each other, they walk around in a big circle, at times even curving their bodies.

behavior   What the animal does, resulting from a cue.

behavior extinction   Withholding *all* reinforcement for a given behavioral response. This will reduce the frequency of the response.

CERF   Canine Eye Registry Foundation. A centralized national registry of dogs that have been certified free of inheritable eye diseases.

consequence   What happens directly after a behavior.

continuous schedule of reinforcement   Giving your dog a treat each and every time he does a correct behavior.

counterconditioning   The use of associative learning to reverse the unwanted effects of prior conditioning.

criteria   What behaviors you will accept from your dog during a particular training session.

desensitization or **systematic desensitization**   A form of counterconditioning; a procedure in which a phobic subject (human or animal) is subjected to low levels of the frightening stimulus while relaxed. The level of frightening stimulus is gradually increased, but never at a rate to cause distress. Eventually the fear dissipates.

redirected aggression   When the dog (or human) takes an emotion he can't express in that situation and directs it toward another object, human, or dog.

dominant   Assertive or pushy, not aggressive. Some dogs (as well as some people) don't know how to take "no" for an answer and will continue to push and push. Many pushy dogs are labeled "dominant" but there are so many definitions of this term and most of them are negative.

glucocorticoids   *See* adrenaline.

hackles   The hair along a dog's spine or neck. A dog's hackles will raise up when he's nervous.

hips and elbows   A dog's hips and elbows need to be checked and certified as sound before he can be bred. If a dog with a history of hip dysplasia or elbow problems is bred, the health problems will be passed along to future generations, causing heartache and pain to the dogs and their humans.

jackpot   Giving the dog lots of treats, all one at a time. I like to give a jackpot when the dog has done something hard for the very first time or if a behavior is particularly wonderful.

learned helplessness   When the dog (or human) just shuts down because nothing he does is ever right. The dog just gives up.

lumping   When you try to train huge portions of a behavior all at the same time; for instance, trying to get a dog to walk on a loose leash for a mile the first time you put a leash on him.

lure   To show with your hands or body posture what you want the dog to do.

neutral stimulus   Something that has no meaning until it's paired with something either positive or negative.

OFA   The Orthopedic Foundation for Animals was formed to help breeders in addressing hip dysplasia and other congenital diseases.

opposition reflex   The natural reflexive action that makes a dog push or pull against anything that is pushing or pulling against him.

precursor   A sign that something is going to happen. This can be a signal that the dog is getting nervous or a sign that something good is going to happen, such as the rattle of a plastic bag, signifying that a dog treat is forthcoming.

Premack principle   The observation that high-probability behavior reinforces low-probability behavior.

provoking stimuli   Things your dog may be afraid of, including people, dogs, cows, horses, fence posts, drain pipes, petting in inappropriate ways, the vacuum cleaner—basically anything that makes the dog nervous.

puppy mill   A place where dogs of many breeds are bred strictly for money. The bitches are kept in deplorable conditions, the puppies are not socialized, and puppies are taken away from mom and littermates entirely too early. There are no health checks on breeding stock, nor on the puppies themselves. "Papers" issued from puppy mills are often fictitious or from unrecognized registries, rendering them useless.

scheduled induced aggression   Angry behavior that results when the results you get don't match your expectations. You know that if you put money in a soda machine, your purchase comes out. If you put money in and nothing comes out, what do you do? You may kick the machine, pound on it, rock it, or grab a sledgehammer and pound it. Why? Because we've learned that putting money into the machine *always* yields us a soda. When it doesn't, we get mad.

scruff shake   Grabbing the dog by the side of the neck, holding him off the ground, and yelling at him.

socialization   A controlled introduction of various situations and things so that the dog develops positive associations with them.

splitting   (1) Breaking a behavior into many small steps and having the dog master one before going on to the next. (2) When two dogs are playing, a third dog will very often run between them to break up what the dog perceives as play that's too rough. Dogs split from the rear for obvious reasons: There are no teeth in the rear.

stimulus   Any event that affects or is capable of affecting behavior.

stimulus control   The dog responds promptly to a cue in any and all situations and doesn't respond with the behavior when it isn't asked for.

systematic desensitization   *See* desensitization.

trial   One repetition of a behavior.

variable schedule of reinforcement   When you sometimes give the dog a treat for a correct behavior and don't other times.

Appendix B

Books and Web Resources

These are the books and websites that I recommend the most if you'd like to learn more about positive training and healthier ways to feed your dogs. I firmly believe that diet affects behavior, so I've also included some of my favorite sources addressing those issues as well.

Books

Booth, Sheila. *Purely Positive Training*. Ridgefield, CT: Podium Publications, 1998.

Billinghurst, Ian. *The Barf Diet*. Bathurst, NSW, Australia: Warrigal Publishing, 2001.

———. *Give Your Dog a Bone*. Bathurst, NSW, Australia: Warrigal Publishing, 1993.

———. *Grow Your Pups with Bones*. Bathurst, NSW, Australia: Warrigal Publishing, 1998.

Brown, Kerry, and Wendy Volhard. *Holistic Guide for a Healthy Dog*. New York: Howell Book House, 1995.

Burch, Mary R., and Jon S. Bailey. *How Dogs Learn*. New York: Howell Book House, 1999.

Chance, Paul. *Learning and Behavior*. 4th ed. Pacific Cove, Calif.: Brooks/Cole, 1999.

Donaldson, Jean. *The Culture Clash*. Berkeley, Calif: James and Kenneth Publishers, 1996.

Lorenz, Konrad. *On Aggression*. Translated by Marjorie Latzke. New York: Routledge, 2002.

Pitcairn, Richard H., and Susan Hubble Pitcairn. *Dr. Pitcairn's Complete Guide to Natural Health for Dogs and Cats*. Emmaus, Pa.: Rodale Press, 1995.

Pryor, Karen. *Don't Shoot the Dog*. Rev. ed. New York: Bantam Books, 1999.

———. *Lads Before the Wind*. Waltham, Mass.: Sunshine Books, 1994.

Reid, Pamela J. *Excel-erated Learning*. Berkeley, Calif: James and Kenneth Publishers, 1996.

Rugaas, Turid. *On Talking Terms with Dogs: Calming Signals*. Carlsborg, Wash.: Legacy by Mail, 1997 (book and video).

Sidman, Murray. *Coercion and Its Fallout*. Boston: Authors Cooperative, 1989.

Spector, Morgan. *Clicker Training for Obedience*. Waltham, Mass: Sunshine Books, 1999.

Websites for Training and General Dog Issues

These are my favorite websites for training and nutrition. There are literally thousands of great sites on the Internet, but there are also thousands of not-great sites. It takes a while to learn how to separate the wheat from the chaff.

Alternate Veterinary Medicine

www.altvetmed.com

Where to find a holistic veterinarian.

American Kennel Club

www.akc.org

Information about breeds, shows, CGC, and other dog sports.

Association of Pet Dog Trainers

www.apdt.com

Australian Shepherd Club of America

www.asca.org

Not just for Aussies! They allow mixed breeds to compete in sanctioned trials.

B-Naturals

www.b-naturals.com

Great source for supplements.

Black Ice

www.blackicedogsledding.com

The only source for X-back sledding harnesses—Pam's pick for the best harness for loose-leash walking!

Bluegrace Portuguese Water Dogs

www.bluegrace.com

A source for alternative medicine—not just for Portuguese Water Dogs!

Cambridge Center for Behavioral Studies

www.behavior.org

Great source for information about behavior in lay terms.

Canine Freestyle Federation, Inc.
www.canine-freestyle.org
Information about Canine Freestyle (dancing with your dog).

Canine Water Sports
www.caninewatersports.com

CERF
www.vet.purdue.edu/~yshen/cerf.html

ClickerSolutions
www.clickersolutions.com
Loads of great information about positive training.

Delta Society
www.deltasociety.org
One of the registries for Therapy Dog work.

Dogwise.com
www.dogwise.com
Where you can get all of the books that are in this listing.

Don't Shoot the Dog!
www.dontshootthedog.com
Karen Pryor's website. Chock-full of great information.

Gary Wilkes' Click & Treat Training
www.clickandtreat.com
Great information on training.

Hearts United for Animals: Puppy Mills
www.hua.org/Prisoners/Puppymills.html
Puppy mill FAQs.

National Association of Dog Obedience Instructors
www.nadoi.org

NaturalRearing.com
www.naturalrearing.com
Information on raising your dog the natural way.

North American Dog Agility Council
www.nadac.com
One of the registries for agility.

Orthodpedic Foundation for Animals (OFA)
www.offa.org

petswelcome.com
www.petswelcome.com
A listing for hotels that accept pets.

Positive Motivation Dog Training
www.positivedogs.com
My website.

SitStay
www.sitstay.com
A great source for the books listed here, plus other pet gear.

Stacy's Wag'N'Train
www.wagntrain.com
Super site with fantastic information about training and behavior.

Thensome pet health: vaccinations
www.thensome.com/vaccinations.htm
Information about vaccinations and how they really aren't needed as often as veterinarians recommend.

Therapy Dogs, Inc.
www.tdi-dog.org
Another registry for Therapy Dog work.

United Kennel Club
www.ukcdogs.com

United States Dog Agility Association
www.usdaa.com
Another registry for agility.

World Canine Freestyle Organization
www.worldcaninefreestyle.org
Another registry for freestyle (dancing with your dog).

Finding a Positive Trainer

So, you're hooked on positive but want some help with the details. There are as many trainers out there with all different levels of expertise and knowledge about learning theory as there are blades of grass. Ask five trainers the best way to train something and you'll get 500 different answers. Many trainers think they are positive; they may use a clicker, but they also use a prong collar. This is *not* positive. This is punishment paired with food.

You'll need to interview your prospective trainer, and these are the questions you should ask:

- How long have you been training?

- What training organizations do you belong to?

- Do you compete in any dog sports? (Not all that important, but I would want to know.)

- What "tools" do you use? (If the answer is prong collars, head halters, and choke collars, *run away.*)

You can even ask pointed questions such as:

- If the dog jumps or bites, what would you recommend? (If the answers are in any way violent or hands-on, *run away.*)

- Can I have references? (Be sure to check them out.)

Ask to observe a few classes. Talk to students after the class. If what you see in the class is disturbing to you, don't join the class. It may take awhile and you may have to drive a further distance than you wanted to, but finding a positive trainer for your best friend will be the best investment you can possibly make.

To find a clicker trainer in your area, check this website:

www.travelvan.net/cgi-bin/marge/mainpage.pl

Appendix C

Training Charts

Make copies of the following charts to use as you practice "Shamu Stays," as discussed in Chapter 14. Use them as you teach the "Sit-Stay," "Down-Stay," and "Stand-Stay." Don't forget that C/T means to click and treat. Although each chart goes up to only Level 8, you can make extra copies if you want to teach longer stays.

Teaching Sit-Stays

Level 1

Say "Sit." Remind at _____ secs.

C/T, release at _____ secs.

Repeat three times, move on to the next time level.

Level 2

Say "Sit." Remind at _____ secs.

C/T, release at _____ secs.

Repeat three times, move on to the next time level.

Level 3

Say "Sit." Remind at _____ secs.

C/T, release at _____ secs.

Repeat three times, move on to the next time level.

Level 4

Say "Sit." Remind at _____ secs.

C/T, release at _____ secs.

Repeat three times, move on to the next time level.

Level 5

Say "Sit." Remind at _____ secs.

C/T, release at _____ secs.

Repeat three times, move on to the next time level.

Level 6

Say "Sit." Remind at _____ secs.

C/T, release at _____ secs.

Repeat three times, move on to the next time level.

Level 7

Say "Sit." Remind at _____ secs.

C/T, release at _____ secs.

Repeat three times, move on to the next time level.

Level 8

Say "Sit." Remind at _____ secs.

C/T, release at _____ secs.

Repeat three times, move on to the next time level.

Teaching Down-Stays

Level 1

Say "Down." Remind at _____ secs.

C/T, release at _____ secs.

Repeat three times, move on to the next time level.

Level 2

Say "Down." Remind at _____ secs.

C/T, release at _____ secs.

Repeat three times, move on to the next time level.

Level 3

Say "Down." Remind at _____ secs.

C/T, release at _____ secs.

Repeat three times, move on to the next time level.

Level 4

Say "Down." Remind at _____ secs.

C/T, release at _____ secs.

Repeat three times, move on to the next time level.

Level 5

Say "Down." Remind at _____ secs.

C/T, release at _____ secs.

Repeat three times, move on to the next time level.

Level 6

Say "Down." Remind at _____ secs.

C/T, release at _____ secs.

Repeat three 3 times, move on to the next time level.

Level 7

Say "Down." Remind at _____ secs.

C/T, release at _____ secs.

Repeat three times, move on to the next time level.

Level 8

Say "Down." Remind at _____ secs.

C/T, release at _____ secs.

Repeat three times, move on to the next time level.

Teaching Stand-Stays

Level 1

Say "Stand." Remind at _____ secs.

C/T, release at _____ secs.

Repeat three times, move on to the next time level.

Level 2

Say "Stand." Remind at _____ secs.

C/T, release at _____ secs.

Repeat three times, move on to the next time level.

Level 3

Say "Stand." Remind at _____ secs.

C/T, release at _____ secs.

Repeat three times, move on to the next time level.

Level 4

Say "Stand." Remind at _____ secs.

C/T, release at _____ secs.

Repeat three times, move on to the next time level.

Level 5

Say "Stand." Remind at _____ secs.

C/T, release at _____ secs.

Repeat three times, move on to the next time level.

Level 6

Say "Stand." Remind at _____ secs.

C/T, release at _____ secs.

Repeat three 3 times, move on to the next time level.

Level 7

Say "Stand." Remind at _____ secs.

C/T, release at _____ secs.

Repeat three times, move on to the next time level.

Level 8

Say "Stand." Remind at _____ secs.

C/T, release at _____ secs.

Repeat three times, move on to the next time level.

Index

D

W-X-Y-Z